AUTISM and the BRAIN ZINNIE

by
Myrrena Schwegmann

ACKNOWLEDGEMENTS

To my editor Kevin Hellon, I need to express great appreciation for going above and beyond any and all expectations to help me reach my goal.

I want to thank Betsy Buck, who provided a great portion of the illustrations.

I want to thank Johnie so much for acknowledging the importance of writing this book despite his desire to have his name withheld.

I want to thank the many friends I have who encouraged this writing despite all the odds. Particularly, Mariana Wells, Jane Wodening, and Darla Stuart.

I want to thank my clients who were all so patient and understanding when Johnie and I were living through it. Nancy, thanks for listening too. We cannot forget dear departed Phil who was an awesome support and even came to one of the IEP meetings.

I want to thank all my family (particularly my daughter Rose), my friends (Jennifer -who even joined me at several meetings, Jeannette, Sherry, Sallie, Carol, etc...), and all my neighbors (Nancy, Rick, Cathy, Jeannie...to name a few), who have patiently been there for us as we explained our horrifying experiences day after day and through all these years.

I want to thank all the new friends I have formed to create that bond and that support that you cannot get from anyone else except the ones who have been there. All my friends who also have children with autism. Thank you Mary and Sandra, my Starbucks buddies!! Thank you Mary, Mariana, Marilyn, and Cyd...or is it Mindy:). Although it is often tough to get together, there is no greater joy than a friend who has been through an awful lot concerning their children, just as you have. Thank you Donna, Pam, Amy, Carolyn, Lynette, Moya and Mark and all others who have been a great support over the years with the familiar understanding of autism and what it is like for our children in the schools.

I apologize right now for the "acronym soup" in my story. It really cannot be avoided. Much of what is written is direct quotes from Johnie's school and medical paperwork. It is also only one of many frustrations I have encountered by being involved in this system and you might as well get the feeling for that too. As you take your journey through the pages of this book, I have provided a cheat-sheet so that it won't be quite so bad for you as it was for me.

ACRONYMS

ASD: Autism Spectrum Disorder

BD: Behavioral Disorder

CBT: Cognitive Behavioral Therapy

CDE: Colorado Department of Educational

DSM-IV: Diagnostic and Statistical Manual for Mental Disorders – Fourth Edition
DX: Diagnosis

ECEA   Exceptional Children's Education Act (rules)

FYI: For Your Information

GT: Gifted/Talented

IDEA: Individuals with Disabilities Education Act

IEE: Independent Education Evaluation

504:   A simpler version of the IEP
IEP: Individualised Education Plan/Program

ILC: Intensive Learning Center

PDD-NOS: Pervasive Development Disorder – Not Otherwise Specified

PE: Physical Educational

R/O: Ruled out

SED: Serious Emotional Disability
SIED: Significant Identifiable Emotional Disorder

SLD: Speech/Language Disability
SLI: Speech/Language Impairment
SLP: Speech/Language Pathologist

WHY I AM WRITING

As a parent of a child with special needs, I am ever so grateful for the creation of the IDEA (Individuals with Disabilities Education Act). Unfortunately, working with the school district, trying to help get my sons needs met and comprehend all of the rules, regulations, protocol, IEP's (Individualized Education Program), diagnostics, legal jargon, and everything else involved with this system, has turned into a very difficult and confusing journey for us.

On our journey, I have met many wonderful people who are helping to make this special needs system work a little better for us all. I have also met many people who have suffered through the maze of confusion that is created by this system. I have met teachers who have quit their jobs and parents who have pulled their children out of the district with no idea where to place them.

Through our experiences, I have come to realize that the parents should not be put into the position of being responsible for making sure that the schools are being accountable. For one thing, parents generally do not have the experience in HOW to make sure the schools are being accountable. Parents do not always know what they need to learn and that can sometimes take years, depending on the parents capability of gaining that knowledge. Parents of special needs kids are incredibly overburdened with the care of their children already.

I believe the Colorado Department of Education needs to have much more of an active role in making sure that the schools are educating our children properly. They already know how to make the schools accountable and should actively check on the schools to see that everything is run appropriately, children are making progress, records are in order, forms are filled out correctly, and the staff is trained properly and accountable for their actions. The biggest mistake I had observed most often was the inability to observe the whole picture, which was preventing the child from getting his needs met. If the child is gifted, he should not be placed in a modified curriculum. If the child has no behavioral problem outside the school district, he cannot have the SED (Serious Emotional Disturbance) label on his IEP (Individualized Education Plan). That is defined by the IDEA rules.

CASE HISTORY: This young 5 year old boy lives with his mother and older sister who all have a very good relationship. His parents are divorced and the boy has supervised visits with his father on Sundays. Visits with his father have been strained because his father suffers with depression due to a brain injury from an auto accident.

As a toddler, the boy lined up his toys in long trains rather than playing with them in the conventional manner. He learned to swim by the time he was three.

Johnie's biggest interest has always been science fiction. He loves to tell imaginary stories of creatures from other worlds. He also loves the computer. He has taught himself how to read, spell, and comprehend math from the "Magic School Bus" computer games, long before he started school.

Johnie's manner is a bit shy, but sweet and friendly. He has the desire to make friends, but often fumbles over the proper etiquette for maintaining a friendship. He is a bit awkward physically and has difficulty keeping up with his peers.

Some behaviors to note. He repeats words and phrases, often out of context to the conversations. Sometimes he has an odd way of communicating or perceiving the conversation and at other times he appears to have brilliant perceptions. He paces (usually on his toes), while flapping or stretching his arms and snapping his fingers. He calls this his "run-around". Even when he is sitting, he will periodically stretch out his arms and snap his fingers for a second or two. This appears to coincide with nervousness or excitement and is particularly notable when he is on the computer.

Johnie struggles with toilet training and has a very hard time getting a proper nights sleep.

Johnie does have age appropriate chores. He cooks his own microwave meals, cleans up after himself and dresses himself. It is important to note that he refuses to wear any clothing with buttons or snaps as he finds them very difficult. The clothing might go on backwards or inside-out once in a while, and the shoes will often be untied and/or he will step on the back of the shoe and wear it like a slipper.

Johnie's family have lovingly agreed that he is not your average kid. He is definitely, one unique kid.

KINDERGARDEN

We had decided as a family to move to a bigger home. Johnie's teenage sister, really wanted a room of her own. The little condo we own was rented and we moved into a double-wide mobile home. This caused Johnie to have kindergarten in two different schools.

Although it was indeed a lovely home with plenty of space for everyone, the situation was most unpleasant in many ways. The schools were not very good and the neighbors were constantly causing us great discomfort. Our kitten was stolen out of our yard. A neighbor boy was in a hit and run car accident. Bickering and unethical behavior was common around us. Worse of all, the location was most inconvenient. So, when the year was up, we moved back into the little condo with the really nice neighbors and the peaceful and good location.

FIRST GRADE

Johnie really loved going to school. He would come home often and teach us all what he had just learned. He still had a problem wetting his pants. Spare clothes were left in his backpack at all times and the teacher made sure that Johnie went to the bathroom every couple of hours. It was the same at home. He complained of bullies now and then. One day, the teacher couldn't help laughing when she called me to report that Johnie and another kid got in trouble for peeing out in the playground.

Teacher comments:

"Handwriting is very large. He leaves no spaces, difficult to read, extra handwriting practice. Difficulty holding pencil, cutting, etc. - letter formation is a concern."

"Does not write about personal experiences like most first graders. He writes about space and out of world experiences."

"He lacks self awareness, usually forgets school bag outside, leaves coat everywhere, can't keep up with school supplies, etc."

"He is very unorganized and has a hard time following classroom routines - ones that have been in place for weeks. He needs lots of reminders. Once he is prompted, he gets right to work."

"Slow processing time - Takes him a couple of minutes to formulate his answers. Sometimes his questions and comments are appropriate, other times they don't make sense."

"He enjoys reading and math is a relative strength."

"Strange hand movements and walks on tip-toes. When he gets excited, he moves his fingers in a rapid motion."

"He is very sweet and gets along well with his peers. Sometimes he does aggravate students by touching them. He gives me a warm smile every day and generally seems to be happy to be at school."

Toward the end of the school year, the teacher called me in for a conference. She had the school social worker with her. They both explained to me that it appeared as if Johnie had Asperger's Syndrome which is a mild form of autism. They must have seen the look of shock on my face, because they both made a great effort to reassure me that it is not a bad thing to have. After all, Bill Gates has it. They sent me out the door with a teachers guide for kids with Aspergers, and a suggestion that I go have the boy officially diagnosed.

When I read the teachers guide, it was most amazing to see how well it described Johnie in so many different ways. It was almost like reading a guide about him. It was then that I was suddenly struck with a realization. In all those years I knew that he was unique, when in fact it was a condition. It took a while for my brain to wrap itself around this different way of perceiving. I spent the summer consuming all the information that I could find on Asperger's Syndrome.

That summer Johnie went sailing with his uncle and took advantage of his sisters new job at Elitches.

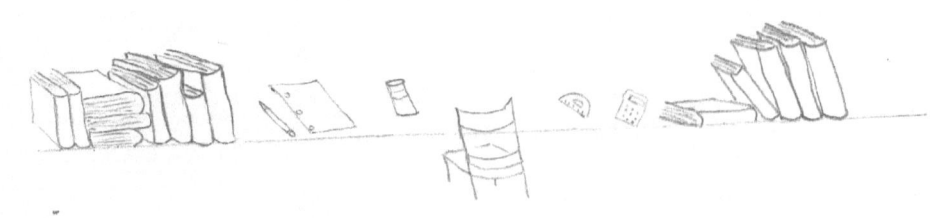

SECOND GRADE

Shortly after school started, I took Johnie in to see the doctor for a diagnosis. She indicated that he did not appear to have Aspergers. This was completely baffling to me because everything that I had read about Asperger's Syndrome, was a very clear description of Johnie I had no idea what to do but just let it go.

Teacher comments:

"He has quite a creative mind. I love hearing his thought process and listening to his stories."

"He is a very creative and thoughtful child. He has shown growth in all academic areas. Continue working on writing."

"He is a gifted writer. Suggested GT (Gifted/Talented) for writing. He is receiving assistance to work on comprehension."

"He is very attentive sometimes, and other times he is at his seat not participating."

"At one time, they were living out of their car."

Parent comment: This is odd. I wonder if it is in reference to when we were living in a mobile home for a year?

"Concerns with him hiding, leaving the room etc. We've also had issues with him taking off at recess."

At school, the teachers helped Johnie with his various needs. He made great headway in all of his academic needs, but coming home daily with concerns about the bullies. As much as his teacher and I had tried to help in any way we could by telling him how to stand up for himself or to avoid the bullies, the situation got worse and worse as the year progressed. Thankfully, that year ended and Johnie could relax with his family for the summer.

Johnie did so well academically, that he was in the gifted/talented program now. Oh, how excited he was to teach us the latest knowledge he had consumed.

THIRD GRADE

Teacher comments:

"I know he's been looked at for the possibility of Asperger's Syndrome. He has some interesting habits that I think are making him feel awkward socially. He does something he calls his runaround. He paces back and forth and does some interesting hand movements. I've attached a letter he wrote explaining why he makes bad choices."

Johnie writes:

"I've been bad. My brain tells me what to do. My body does it too. I do a thing called runaround. it's where you walk while you think. I'll do better next time."

Parent comment: Johnie is harming no one and is not behaving badly. What exactly are his bad choices? Shouldn't she be teaching the children tolerance and acceptance of others differences?

Right after Johnie wrote this note, he started hitting the ever present bullies. When he was asked why he was hitting the kids, he said, "It was a glitch." After this happened several times, I finally pulled him out of school and took him to the hospital.

I was not as concerned about the way he was speaking as the teachers were. I knew he had an odd way of speaking sometimes and that he most likely gleaned the reference of "glitches" from the Walt Disney movie that had come out recently called "Lilo and Stitch: Stitch has a Glitch." I was far more concerned with why he would be aggressive for the first time in his life.

After several days in the hospital, the doctors had agreed on a diagnosis of Psychosis. This was a shock to our whole family. Wasn't it obvious that he had no signs of psychosis at all? What is the confusion? I agreed to start him on the recommended medication and put him in the day program at the hospital

if they assessed Johnie for Asperger's Syndrome. They never did.

During that time, I did quite a bit of research on psychosis to discover why Johnie was being misdiagnosed. I did notice the more I read that he had no signs of psychosis and all the signs of Asperger's Syndrome. We could all clearly see that the boy was simply having difficulties understanding the line of questioning that the doctors had subjected him to. Another thing that was really fascinating, was that the two diagnostics have a very interesting history and connection together. Here are just a few observations.

* Before 1970, all autism was diagnosed as childhood psychosis.

* Because children with autism have a difficult time comprehending language pragmatics and socialization issues, they are still today, often confused with psychosis simply because they do not know how to communicate well.

- Children also tend to enjoy a bit of fantasy now and then. They have not developed the cognitive abilities to permit them to observe and compare their experiences in an objective manner.

PLEASE NOTE: Johnie is extraordinarily interested in fantasy as we have already become aware of. His interest is at such a high level, that several teachers have pointed out his amazing creativity and gifted quality in writing and/or telling his fantasy stories. This interest in fantasy is what led to his interest in the movie "Lilo and Stitch: Stitch has a Glitch." You see, Stitch is a creature from another planet.   That is where Johnie learned to speak of his feelings as glitches.

I sat down with Johnie and asked him, "What is a glitch?"

"Bad thoughts", he said.

"Of what?" I asked him.

"The bullies", he replied.

From my perspective, Johnie was simply trying to explain the overwhelming anger he felt toward the bullies. That rage that caused a "glitch", or an inability to hold back on the desire to punch them. So, I spent a great deal of time teaching him about emotions and how to explain them, what they look like, what they feel like and acting them out just for the fun of it. The lessons worked perfectly. Within a very short time, he had no need to talk about glitches because he now knew how to explain his thoughts and feelings in the appropriate way.

This whole situation happened shortly after Johnie was punished for doing his run-around. This appeared significant to me because he is not normally aggressive and uses his run-around for self-calming. I do not think the teacher had any idea that she had taken away his only means of self calming. His ability to refrain from the desire to punch the bullies who were always so mean to him, was taken away that day. I spoke to Johnie about how hitting others would make him a bully too. I knew that he did not want to be a bully, and there has never been a report of him hitting anyone ever again after that.

Teacher comments: We have discussed in our team meeting that Johnie certainly is experiencing some behaviors that we need to keep an eye on. I've recommended him for a social group. He appears to have slipped through the cracks, and we want to make sure he gets what he needs.

Needless to say, The staff at school were at a loss. It was unclear what Johnie's needs were at that time. They eventually told me that he really needs an IEP. "What is that ?" I asked. When children have special needs in the schools, an Individualised Education Program is initiated to indicate all of his needs on a form for the teachers to be able to refer to when needed.

THE IEP (Individualised Education Program)

Teacher comments:

"Academic skills, basic reading skills and broad written language scores are all well above average."

"Johnie may understand instruction and repeat them back to the teacher, but may not know how to complete a given task within a prescribed time frame. These are skills he is likely acquiring in small groups such as his gifted/talented group."

"Johnie is well above grade level in math. His ability to work out problems mentally, was actually fun to observe."

"While Johnie may have been socially awkward at school, he was never a behavior problem. He is a very compliant and cooperative child."

"Johnie continues to experience his glitches. He has a difficult time not talking about them at school and often goes to the school nurse for physical ailments caused by the glitches."

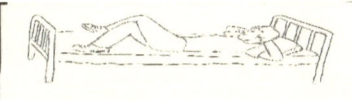

" Johnie is compliant, cooperative and respectful.....Consequences that work well for Johnie when he is misbehaving, is time out and loss of privileges. While he will argue the initial consequence, he accepts the consequence well. Among other things, he loves to play chess and participates in Cub Scouts."

Johnie demonstrated a right pencil grasp which appeared somewhat awkward, as he showed a partially open web space and his middle finger remained extended. It is recommended that he continue to receive motor support."

Johnie was cooperative and compliant throughout the testing. He demonstrated confidence in his own ability and worked very hard. He does need additional time to process information and could benefit from additional time to finish work at home and school."

DETERMINATION OF DISABILITY – SIED (Significant Identifiable Emotional Disability)

I had never been to an IEP meeting before and my understanding of some of the things up for discussion were vague at best. I had no idea what SIED meant, but I trusted the teachers to know what was best for the boy in the school. It sure looked like the teachers did a really good job of testing him.

In the following months, I was called to come pick up Johnie so often, that I did finally begin to wonder if the IEP was as effective at taking care of his needs as I was led to believe. While things appeared to be getting progressively worse for him at school, he was achieving many goals and learning quite a bit at home and in his community.

Johnie went to Cub Scouts once a week that school year and was very excited every time he reached the goal of winning a badge, a pin, a patch, or a belt loop.

Johnie had a paper stuck on the fridge that showed emotions, so that if he got stuck not knowing how to explain something, he could refer back to it. He also asked about a million questions. Some of them so difficult, that I had to tell him to "google it". One time for a joke, he typed in "google it" and got google in Italian.

The most wonderful thing that happened that year, was that he finally - after four years of trying - finally learned to ride his bike. I could see that he was unable to learn to ride in the conventional way. I had read at one time that Aspies (People who have Asperger's Syndrome), have a difficult time comprehending and sometimes need to learn the "parts before the whole". I knew that Johnie was struggling to learn how to do it all at once . I bought him a pair of heelies (A popular shoe at the time with wheels on the heels), and taught him to balance, then roll, then steer, etc. After about a month, he had mastered the heelies and I put him back on his bicycle to try again. In five minutes, he was a bit wobbly, but he was riding all on his own. What a glorious day that was!! Johnie rode and rode that bike all summer long and yes, he got his Cub Scout badge for that achievement too!!!

FOURTH GRADE IEP

Teacher comments:

"He is a very pleasant child who loves to learn"

"He is very intelligent and has tested in the above average range of intelligence. In the past, he participated in th....."

Parent comments:

"It is strange that this sentence was never finished. I can see where the teacher is headed and that the sentence should end with, the Gifted/Talented program. Perhaps the teacher realized a gifted child should never be placed into a modified curriculum. This plan was never explained to me. As far as I knew, he was being placed into a smaller sized classroom with proper academic challenges. This situation became one more added stress for Johnie He did not see the point of going to that school because he wasn't receiving an education at all."

Teacher comments:

SPEECH THERAPY -Using fluent speech, expressing self with age appropriate vocabulary and grammar. Following and giving directions, and demonstrating appropriate use of voice and vocal quality. "No concerns in communication abilities at this time."

Parent comments:

"At home it has always been quite obvious that Johnie struggles with communication abilities. His first grade teacher had made a note of this struggle. If there are no concerns in communication, why has another teacher described all kinds of communication issues right on this IEP? Please continue reading"

Teacher comments:

In October, Johnie began talking about glitches and their need to be physically aggressive. At this time he is talking about these glitches at least once a day."

Parent comment:

"This is a concern in communication abilities. Remember, Johnie explained that glitches are bad thoughts, so I taught him to explain his thoughts and feelings in the appropriate way more than a year ago. Why is Johnie still explaining his feelings as glitches, here in school? I have read in a number of books that people with Aspergers have difficulties generalizing their knowledge. It looks to me as if Johnie knows how to explain his thoughts and feelings at home but hasn't figured out how to explain in the same way at school. Why? Because he knows that is what they expect of him at school? I really don't know but it does appear to be a case of being unable to generalize his knowledge."

Teacher comments:

"Johnie often struggles with peer relationships. He plays well, but sometimes gets frustrated when he is unable to express how he is feeling."

Parent comments:

"Again, this is a concern in his communication abilities. Obviously he has tried other techniques to try to express his feelings besides the glitches and those have not worked either. I am working double time to teach the boy how to communicate and the teachers have no comprehension that it is a need. Are these teachers qualified to make determinations of a child's needs?"

Teacher comments:

" On 9/12/06, Johnie brought a steak knife to school with the intention of hurting himself. He has also asked his classmates to hurt him on multiple occasions."

Parent comment:

"Actually, this is another concern about his communication abilities. Johnie was NOT trying to hurt himself. He was trying to show the bullies how they were hurting him. He also tried to explain to his classmates that they were hurting him. Again, he is showing us that he is unable to know how to express his feelings in an appropriate manner."

Teacher comments:

As a consequence for bringing a knife to school, Johnie received a two day suspension. Within 15 minutes of his return to school, he had another episode."

Parent comment:

"I am now very concerned that there is an awful lot of attention to the behaviors of Johnie with absolutely no attention to WHY the behavior is happening. You see, I had difficulties at times understanding what the boy is trying to say, but I cared enough to be patiently persistent. I learned that Johnie had written a note to a girl telling her how much he liked her. When he gave the note to the girl, she rejected him and a bunch of the kids got a big kick out of the situation and teased the heck out of Johnie He couldn't go tell the teacher because they never did anything and anyway, he would be bullied all the more for tattling. If he tried walking away from the heckling, they would usually follow him. When he tried to stick up for himself last year by punching the bullies, HE got in trouble for that. When he tried bringing a knife to school or choking himself (the episode), to show the bullies that they are hurting him, again HE gets in trouble. The Bully-proofing system did not work for him. He simply did not understand it.

Teacher comments:

"Johnie has been seen in the office numerous times after leaving his classroom without permission. It was explained to him that he was not allowed to do this because of safety issues however, it continued to occur."

Parent comments:

"Instead of telling Johnie that he must not do that, which is obviously not working, wouldn't it be wiser to find out WHY it is happening so that they can create a solution?

Teacher comments:

Psychotic Disorder NOS (Not Otherwise Specified)

R/O PDD NOS (ruled out – Pervasive Development Disorder – Not Otherwise Specified)

"He is currently on Risperdal for the psychotic symptoms and Prozac was recently added to address the anxiety and depression."

Parent comments:

The hospital added PDD NOS (This diagnosis is given to people with mild autism when the doctor is unsure of where on the spectrum that person fits). They did not rule it out. Was the school ruling it out? WHY? I agreed to give my son Risperidal because it is often given to kids with Asperger's. The side affects were good and bad. It caused him to get very hungry and inevitably gain some extra weight. It also helped him sleep through the night. This turned out to be an incredible relief because he always had a very hard time getting a good nights sleep. The addition of Prozak caused me a high degree of anger. Why is my son only able to survive school if he is on an anti-depressant? Why are the schools so unsafe for him? Who is helping my son feel safe in the schools?"

Teacher comments:

The boys mother is not fully in agreement with the diagnosis of psychosis. She believes that the boy is frequently bullied and gets very anxious.

Parent comments:

They forgot to mention that I know my son well enough to know that he has Asperger's Syndrome which is in direct relation to why he is frequently bullied and over anxious. I have also stated that my son shows no signs of psychosis... obviously.

Teacher comments:

Currently, the boy is receiving few support services. He has 30 minutes a week with the mental health providers and 15 minutes a week with the special education teacher for reading comprehension.

Parent comments:

Johnie was far more stressed than ever before. I found myself pulling him out of school on numerous occasions. He didn't understand the behavioral lessons. He did not understand the behavior of the teachers. He did not understand the behavioral or social lessons from the teachers. There was no comprehension of why they would not give him challenging schoolwork. He was learning poor behavior from his peers and associating stress with learning. I had to pull him out of school and let him do his work at home for a couple of days to get back that joy in learning that he had always had before. He did not see the point of going to that school at all. I called district and they agreed to send the Autism Team to do an assessment on Johnie. I also found a doctor to do another diagnosis.

The doctor again gave him a diagnosis of psychosis. In frustration, I told the doctor that Johnie does not show any signs of psychosis and he would need to send proof that Johnie's run-around (for example) is any indication of "severe psychosis" (as he wrote).

In a few days, I did indeed receive the diagnosis with an attached printout entitled "Psychosis in Childhood and it's Management". The attachment he sent, described in many details how it is very important to be careful about diagnosing psychosis in children and particularly if those children might have Aspergers. All the things that I had already said to him and to many people at the schools.

11-16-07 Autism Team Referral Form
Team reports:

Distorted thinking, ie feeling hypnotism was happening in the class because some of the students seemed happy.

Parent comment:

Please refer to the communication section (pages 21—22), where you can see how distorted this observation really is.

Team reports:

Current behaviors include passive noncompliance with adult request to stop doing something, he will state he needs to get up to do a walk-around (related to anxiety), which he does by walking to the bathroom.

Parent comment:

This is clearly in reference to his run-around which the Autism Team should be familiar with as it is a common characteristic of kids with autism. It is his repetitive mannerism that is often technically called "stimming." It is not related to anxiety unless he is using it to calm himself from anxiety. He also uses it to express joy and excitement.

Team reports:

Has difficulty expressing his feelings. When given feedback about a behavior, can become anxious, distorting the adult intent, i.e. telling mom the teacher was mad at him.

Parent comment:

The social aspect of being unable to know how to express his feelings is common with kids who have ASD like Johnie. I have always pointed out that the teachers tone of voice should not in any way be elevated if they want to communicate well with him. Johnie cannot hear if the teacher is too loud or too firm. This is a clear sign of Auditory Sensory Sensitivity which is also a common characteristic of children on the autism spectrum.

Team reports:

Current DX (Diagnosis):   PDD-NOS & Psychosis.

Parent comment:

It is odd that the Autism Team is completely ignoring the diagnosis of and the symptoms of autism. A person has to question WHY?

Autism Team comments on their diagnostic assessment:

No evidence for an ASD (Autism Spectrum Disorder), no criteria were met. Amidst considerable, cumulative stresses - including to but not limited to, a sense of and fear of being bullied by peers, concerns about interpersonal rejection by peers, and increased time spent with his father (an issue he is extremely confused and conflicted about) – Johnie did develop a process of atypical thinking.....While it appears he did have a thought disorder at that time, this does not currently appear to be the case....Johnie is a youngster who wants to do well, and herein lies a piece of the dilemma: His feelings of anger and suspiciousness toward others feels alien and distasteful to him. Johnie is certainly an at risk youngster, with an emotional disability, who requires a supportive and structured educational milieu. It is strongly recommended that he remain in a behavioral developmental program within the district.

Parent comments:

I had expressed my appreciation of the assessment but suggested that Johnie should have been assessed in a different location. It is very clear that he should NOT remain in the behavioral developmental program because it was not useful behaviorally or academically to him with his needs. I could agree on one sentence and only one that was written that really sums up quite clearly WHY Johnie must leave the program. "HIS FEELINGS OF ANGER AND SUSPICIOUSNESS TOWARDS OTHERS FEELS ALIEN AND DISTASTEFUL TO HIM."

Johnie has clearly never been in this type of environment and should never have been placed there. This assessment notes a diagnosis, i.e. "no ASD" (Autism Spectrum Disorder), even though their Referral Form notes a diagnosis of ASD, and many symptoms, but does not specify WHAT his needs are. Most alarming of all is that the Autism Team does not know how to identify an ASD. It also notes that Johnie has trouble with bullies and suggests that he remain in the same program where he is surrounded by bullies. How does that make professional sense?

I did a lot more research that year. Something was seriously wrong with how Johnie is assessed. They appear to be talking about and working with an entirely different kid than I have always known. So, I researched child development, SIED. IEP, IDEA, Advocacy, etc.... I lodged a complaint against the BD teachers in that school. I also received something by email that seemed to fit right in to our situation and I sent it along with. This is what I received:

ARE YOU A BULLY?

By Linda Starr

Classroom management, according to education expert Harry Wong, is the "practices and procedures that allow teachers to teach and students to learn."

Bullying, according to Dictionary.com is the practice of being "habitually cruel or overbearing, especially to smaller or weaker people."

In other words, those who can, manage their classrooms. Those who can't, manage their students. The former are educators; the latter are bullies. And, believe me, you can tell the difference.

Educators let students know they care.

Bullies let students know who's boss.

Educators teach self control.

Bullies exert their own control.

Educators set ironclad expectations.

Bullies rule with whims of steel.

Educators diffuse minor disruptions with humor.

Bullies use sarcasm to turn disruptions into confrontations.

Educators privately counsel chronic discipline problems.

Bullies publicly humiliate chronic misbehavers.

Educators are judicious.

Bullies are judgmental.

Educators, aware of the power they wield over their students, choose their words and actions carefully.

Bullies wield their power recklessly, frequently resorting to anger and intimidation.

Educators help all students feel successful.

Bullies punish students for being unsuccessful.

-18-

Educators address misbehavior.

Bullies attack the character of the misbehaviors.

Educators see each student's uniqueness.

Bullies compare children to one another.

Educators treat all students with respect.

Bullies make it clear that not all students deserve respect.

Educators highlight good behavior.

Bullies make examples of poor behavior.

Educators are proactive; they create classroom environments that minimize student behavior.

Bullies are reactive; they blame students for the lack of order in their classrooms.

Educators educate.

Bullies humiliate.

Educators exude confidence in their ability to maintain order in their classrooms.

Bullies barely conceal their terror of losing control.

Are you a bully?

IDEA (The Individuals with Disabilities Education Act)

Although I was familiar with medical terms and found reading medical books relatively simple because of some medical training in my past, the IDEA rules felt quite a bit more daunting a read because it was more legal in nature. However, it did appear obvious that quite a few rules had already been broken.

Johnie does not fit the SED (Serious Emotional Disability) label.

He clearly fits the autism label.

He is not getting a free, appropriate public education.

He is in an incredibly restricted environment.

There is no parent participation no matter what the effort has been.

ADVOCACY

It was recommended by many that I needed to get an advocate to help me work with the schools and make sure they are accountable for taking care of my sons needs.

As Johnie had a diagnosis of psychosis, there are no advocacy organizations that could help. ARC works with people who have a developmental disability. They were willing to help provide an advocate based on the discharge papers that indicated PDD-NOS. However, when Johnie was again misdiagnosed with psychosis in fourth grade, we lost our advocate. We were all alone again and helpless, facing a bureaucracy that does not work.

COMMUNICATION

Johnie could speak quite well but sometimes you could tell that he did not always know how to communicate or comprehend very well and had a very literal view on things. In my research on child development, I was quite interested to note that right about the age when he started having problems in school, is when children are learning far more complex forms of communication. While all of his peers were intuitively learning to read body language and non-verbal cues, etc. he was even more clueless than he was ever before. Here are a few of our challenges:

Story one: I am driving around town with Johnie.

Mom: "Dang, I keep hitting red lights."

Johnie: "What do you mean?"

Mom: "Well, I keep getting red lights."

Johnie: "I don't see you hitting or getting lights. What do you mean?"

Mom: "Oh I see. I mean that I have to keep stopping at red lights."

Story two: I went to pick up Johnie from a friends house and chatted with the friends mother for a bit. She told an interesting story. She had asked Johnie to show her the front of the book. For affect, the woman stuck her tongue out of the side of her mouth to show concentration as she is demonstrating how he had taken the book and twisted it this way and that way for a while as he is trying to figure out how to show her the front of the book. Finally, he proudly showed her the paper edge of the book. He must have concluded that the spine was the back of the book as you see it on a bookshelf.

Story three: One day Johnie called me while I was at work.

Johnie: "I hurt my finger when I jabbed it in paint."

Mom: "You did? I am sorry that you hurt yourself." As I was reassuring him, I was also trying very hard to discern what he meant because there were no cans of paint laying around the house and if there were, how could he hurt himself if he stuck his finger in the paint. Finally, my mind came up with the only possibility I could think of even though it was rather a long shot.

Mom: "Was the paint on the wall?"

Johnie: "Yes. When I was running down the stairs, I jammed my finger in the paint on the wall and it hurt."

While we had fun with his communication difficulties in his personal life, at school and in the doctors offices, it became very confusing and downright creepy at times. Read on.

One day Johnie came home from school and spoke to me about his frustration of the day.

Johnie: "The teachers are hypnotizing us."

Mom: "What do you mean?"

Johnie: "Their trying to hypnotize us."

Mom: "How?"

Johnie: "By telling us to smile all the time."

Mom: "How is that hypnotizing?"

Johnie: "Because they keep telling us to smile when we don't feel like it."

I went to the school to try to make some sense of that situation because it was happening all the time and becoming quite frustrating for Johnie Two staff members met with me and insisted that he was trying to manipulate me against them. I know for starters that my son simply does not think that way. He is far more passive than that. I explained that he does not know how to manipulate. He is too naive, too self centered to think that way. Manipulation is a complicated form of communication that he has never learned. For some reason, they were very angry and did not even give me the chance to explain WHY he felt like they were trying to hypnotize. It was very creepy that these teachers had no desire to communicate or even begin to understand.

The doctor wrote: "Johnie shared that he believed that his school was hypnotizing him. Their trying to control me. They use their mind to make me do something. They put thoughts into your head and make you do them...."

Again, the WHY factor is completely missing in the report which makes it appear as if it is something really creepy.

I could see that the way in which many of the professionals were communicating with Johnie was a serious problem. They often asked leading questions that he could not understand and they were not determining WHY a situation, a behavior or a statement was said. This was causing a great deal of confusion and stress for Johnie and for all of us. I tried very hard to explain that, to no avail. Nobody wanted to hear me. I am no professional, but am I a mother in denial of her sons condition? It would appear as if the schools had every right to be downright frustrated at me because I would not stop telling them that my son has Asperger's Syndrome when all the diagnostic reports so far, show psychosis. But wait just one minute, wouldn't I be considered an authority of him? After all, I have known him all his life. I know him better than anyone. Plus, lets not forget that the boys teachers in first and second grade could see that the boy had Aspergers too.

There were now three diagnostic reports stating that I do not know what I am talking about and yet, I never gave up. I had done far too much research. I knew too much. Aspergers runs in our family. My half-brother has it which helps me know without doubt that I know what I am dealing with. I knew how to read diagnostic reports, medical books, the DSM IV, etc. I could see in many aspects what the professionals were doing wrong. Much of it was laziness. It takes an awful lot of work to do a diagnosis for Asperger's Syndrome. The first doctor reported that the boy didn't have it, and you can see that she did not do the appropriate testing for Asperger's Syndrome. The other doctors did not even bother to read that diagnosis. They just saw that he was tested there already and let it go at that.

BRAIN ZINNIE

Johnie has a history of running from various situations. He has run away from people if they hollered or talked too much. He has often run from classrooms and the playground. Even at family parties where he is really enjoying himself, he often feels a need to leave early.

When we asked him why he kept running away, he said that too much commotion causes a BRAIN ZINNIE: It is the physical feeling of the body shutting down, as in an inability to think or hear anything anymore due to the loud noises or commotion in the immediate area. Retreat to a quiet area (like a nurses office at school or the bedroom at home), is the best way to get back in touch with ones self. It is a matter of survival.

In Tim Page's book "Parallel Play", he wrote about a similar experience: "Eventually, I realized that I could go to the nurse's office if I became overstimulated. It was quiet there, and I could lie down in a darkened room and be alone, and soon I would make any excuse I could to find that peace. Some of my teachers thought this was a ploy for attention. I have since concluded that it was, in fact, a survival tactic, for it allowed me to try to settle my own hubbub, away from the jangling, jarring hubbub of others."

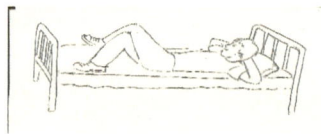

In Temple Grandin's book "The Way I See It", She explains: "Sensory overload can cause either vision or hearing to shut down completely. During these times, no information will get through to the brain, and learning will not occur."

SUMMER

By the end of fourth grade, we were all quite relieved for the approaching summer vacation. No more worries about finding an advocate. No worries about what Johnie's label was or how he should be taught or what services he is getting. We could relax and be normal. He spent a lot of time with his friends from cub scouts and even took one of them sailing with his uncle for a week.

Johnie was still having difficulties wetting the bed at night. Once summer started, he had no problems with that dilemma. Unfortunately, he was back to wetting the bed again when school started in the fall.

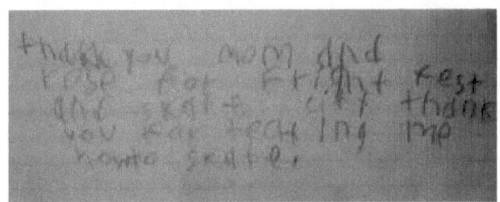

My favorite book at the time was Tony Atwood's "The Complete Guide to Asperger's Syndrome. This book (among other sources), helped me know that I was not the problem. Every page clearly describes my sons difficulties in school and how to help him and I did everything I could to explain those details.

He wrote: "A child with Asperger's Syndrome may also create his or her own words or neologisms. This ability to provide a novel perspective on language is fascinating, and one of the endearing and genuinely creative aspects of Asperger's syndrome.

I am grateful to note that he is giving a positive view (as his family always has), on Johnie's use of his words.

He writes: "Hans Asperger was keen to differentiate autistic personality disorder from schizophrenia, and noted that, While the schizophrenic patient seems to show progressive loss of contact, the children we are discussing lack contact from the start."

Children with Asperger's Syndrome may develop what appear to be signs of paranoia, but this may be an understandable response to very real social experiences. They encounter a greater degree of deliberate and provocative teasing than their peers....

A study shows that the paranoia due to the impaired Theory of Mind abilities of a person with Asperger's Syndrome, was qualitatively different to the characteristics of paranoia observed in people with a diagnosis of schizophrenia. The paranoia was not a defense strategy, as occurs in schizophrenia, but due to confusion in understanding the subtleties of social interaction and social rules.

Another problem with the pragmatic and semantic aspects of language that occurs with people who have AS, is that they often make a literal interpretation of a question. A psychiatrist may ask a question such as "Do you hear voices?" A person with AS would answer the question correctly as "Yes." They literally hear voices of people talking around them all day.

Please note that Mr. Attwood does an awesome job of explaining just what happened to my son in one diagnostic evaluation after the next. This helped me cope with the conflicting viewpoints I was getting from several sources in the school district.

FIFTH GRADE

FIRST IEP

Teacher comments:

"The family is currently seeking outside assessment and an additional meeting will be held once that is complete."

"Johnie has not discussed his glitches, however he continues to make social mistakes that cause him to be a target of teasing or ostracizing by his fellow students."

Parent comments:

Isn't it interesting that this teacher is now making the connection that Johnie's discussions of the glitches are a "social mistake."

DIAGNOSIS

I was able to convince the insurance company of how important it was for Johnie to be assessed by a specialist because of the conflicting reports to date. Primarily, I had pointed out that the last doctor had diagnosed my son with severe psychosis and a month later, the Autism Team had shown no signs of psychosis at all.

The specialist we went to did an awesome job. She spent many hours working with Johnie and even observed him in the school. The report was by far the most comprehensive, clear and well written diagnostic assessment on him, ever written. He finally received a diagnosis of Asperger's Syndrome.

She even explained her observations of some of the diagnostic reports that Johnie had received to date. "The (first) report indicates difficulties with eye contact, language and auditory processing delays, social skills delays, problems with transitions, rigid behaviors and sensory-motor problems, including toe walking and fine motor delays. She reported the results of a physical exam and interview, but no autism specific testing was conducted. She ruled out a diagnosis of Aspergers but did not give any reasoning for doing so. She recommended an Occupational, Speech and Physical Therapy evaluation."

"According to the (second) report, the hospital ruled out Aspergers because it was previously ruled out by the first doctor. He was not given any specific testing for Aspergers. He was diagnosed with psychosis due to his talk about glitches and his ability to describe them when asked what they look like, said and did. The report describes interpersonal difficulties, social withdrawal, difficulties processing information, rigidity, and a lack of awareness of social norms."

Parent comment:

It was such a relief to finally be able to go get an advocate. We were unable to find an advocate to help us when Johnie was misdiagnosed. The confusions created by the schools is a daunting task for me or any parent to try to make sense of on our own.

SECOND IEP

SIED label: One or both of the following characteristics shall be present.

ACADEMIC FUNCTIONING: An inability to receive reasonable educational benefit from regular education which is not primarily the results of intellectual, sensory, or other health factors, but due to the identified emotional condition.

Parent comments:

In the last two years, the academic functioning of a child with SIED was marked, even though Johnie's academic capabilities were well above average as reported in both IEPs. Through my persistence, they did not mark it this year.

SOCIAL/EMOTIONAL FUNCTIONING: An inability to build or maintain interpersonal relationships which significantly interferes with the child's social development. Social development involves those adaptive behaviors and social skills which enables a child to meet environmental demands and assume responsibility for his/her own and others welfare.

Teacher comments:

"Playing well with other children."

"Sharing and respecting the rights of others."

"Johnie does have some friends here at school that he enjoys and that enjoy him."

"Interactions with these peers demonstrate an age appropriate desire to be liked and included."

"It is the opinion of this clinician, given the assessments and observations of the boy, that his characteristics are not consistent with the DSM-IV (Diagnostic and Statistical Manual of Mental Disorders – Fourth Edition) criteria for Asperger's Disorder. Indeed, he has developed some nice relationships at this school.

Parent comments:

" Isn't it rather shocking that all these teachers have pointed out over and over again that the boy does not fit the criteria for the social/emotional dysfunction that would require an SIED label on this IEP, and yet they insisted on it." My persistence even with an advocate present was fruitless despite the evidence. It is interesting to note that Johnie only had one friend for a short while in this school year. Are the teachers trying to show that Johnie does not fit the criteria for Aspergers? They do not appear to be fully aware of what the criteria for Aspergers is. Their attempt to show that he does not fit the criteria for Aspergers, has caused them to show he does not fit the criteria for SIED either.

Teacher comments:

"Johnie sometimes struggles to relate and fit in with his peers. He often waits for others to initiate conversation and sometimes tries to get peoples attention through inappropriate comments or actions. He has told other students or made gestures about sticking rocks and balls up his bottom. He has invited himself to parties or followed someone around too closely in an apparent attempt to bond. He has even slammed his body into others at recess in an apparent attempt to fit in with the boys."

"Johnie exhibits a behavior that he calls 'the run-around' where he jumps forward and back, waving his arms in the air."

Parent comments:

Believe it or not, all these comments are written on the same IEP as above. They also show the communication and social failings and the repetitive mannerisms of a child with Aspergers as defined by the DSM-IV (Diagnostic and Statistical Manual for Mental Disorders- Forth Edition).

Teacher comments:

"Johnie appears to use avoidance to cope with stress. His classroom teacher has noticed that he wants to return to the BD (Behavioral Disorder) room following a conflict with other students or when he is held accountable for his behavior. He has class breaks he can use and often seems to use them when there is challenging schoolwork to be done."

Parent comment:

"Needing a quiet place to go when a person is stressed does not appear to me to be avoidance. It sounds like the perfect thing to do."

Teacher comments:

"The district and Johnie's mother have agreed that he struggles in three main areas including social relationships, functional school organization, and stress management."

Parent comment:

"These are some of the most notable difficulties that a child with Aspergers will have in a school

environment as defined by the teachers guide that I have passed out to all of the boys teachers, every year.

The "clinician" who made the statement that Johnie does not fit the diagnostic criteria for Aspergers on this IEP, is not even qualified to make that notation. She was an SLP (Speech/Language Pathologist) This, and the diagnosis done by the Autism Team last year, both show clear diagnostic evaluations and yet they insist that they are just doing assessments.

I have presented the staff and the Autism Team with a diagnosis that was written by a specialist who has done all the appropriate testing for Aspergers and provided that diagnosis. I was in shock to note that the people in this district seem to feel they know more and/or are more qualified to know a child's needs than a specialist or even the child's mother. If they were just doing assessments, they would not be focusing on the label, but on the needs of the boy.

Teacher comments:

"Johnie is able to remember and follow step by step directions."

"Johnie's difficulties lie in his ability to follow oral direction."

"Johnie often misses oral directions and does not appear to hear what you say to him."

Parent comment:

"The teachers appear to have very conflicting observations of Johnie's capabilities. This makes it difficult to see what their qualifications for assessing the boy are."

Teacher comments:

"Johnie often writes about fantasy subjects that include someone getting hurt or someone hurting others. These writing should continue to be monitored and shared with the psychologist as needed."

Parent comment:

In first and second grade, his fantasy stories were described as "gifted" and "very creative". Now it is described as something really creepy. Again, I must question the qualifications and/or capabilities of the staff in assessing my sons needs.

FEELING THE COMMOTION

We moved to this district the year that Johnie was born and his sister was in fifth grade. From the beginning it was obvious that this was a good school system and we always carried a torch of pride because our children were attending school in this district.

When Johnie started school, there was nothing to complain about. As the family is learning more and more about AS and psychosis, it appears as if the staff at school are doing the best they can for him.

By the time That Johnie had started fourth grade, our research had included childhood development. Using what we had learned about Asperger's Syndrome in our daily lives, had made living with Johnie much easier as we were learning how to work with him. He was also learning more as we were able to teach him more than we could before. That is when we knew for a fact that he had AS. There was no question anymore.

As our personal lives were getting easier and easier, the schools were getting more and more difficult and confusing. That is when it became blatantly obvious that Johnie was not the problem. It was the teachers, not helping him at school.

The flaming torch that we carried so many years for that school district, slowly fizzled out as Johnie endured one confusing, humiliating and painful situation after the next until there was nothing more than a puff of smoke at years end when the Autism Team had finished their diagnostic evaluation.

In the months that followed, I did everything I could think of to light that torch again. I wrote long letters of explanations and finally got another diagnosis for Aspergers's Syndrome, from a specialist this time. We had very high hopes and we knew this would solve everything. We set up an IEP meeting to change the label to AS on the IEP, so that Johnie could receive the proper care and finally get his needs met..

At that meeting: "On my right is the social worker who is whispering snide comments which I must answer, 'No ma'am, not true.' (She is mad at me because I tried to explain to her several months ago that her social skills class is inappropriate for Johnie and that he could not go to them anymore.) On my left, is our advocate, who is sitting quietly. On her left is the school principal, who is trying hard to lean over to hear the snide comments. On her left are two people from district. The first one was not invited because he worked on the Autism Team and appeared to have no interest in paying attention to the needs of Johnie He contributed now and again throughout the meeting anyway. The other person glowered at me the whole time with her arms crossed tightly across her chest. The rest of the people are all a blur but I remember there were so many people that they wouldn't all fit at the table.

Someone hands me a paper that the boy has written to show me how well he can write. It must have taken him an hour and a lot of patience on the teachers part to create that. I have never seen anything so neat and legibly written by the boy before that day or since. I was shown another paper which showed the IEP label as SIED and not AS.

The air is thick with frustration and anger all around me. I am numb and everything becomes foggy. I couldn't hear anymore. I couldn't think anymore. I am wondering if this is what Johnie feels in a room full of commotion. I am wondering if I am experiencing a Brain Zinnie.

The torch that I had tried so hard to light, fell to the floor with a thud. Ashes float around for a while and settle onto the floor under our feet causing black smears no different than what I felt in my heart."

Mom (to social worker): Johnie is not old enough or mature enough yet (primarily because of his disability), to know how to control his emotions. You are an adult and a social worker. Those who depend on you, expect you to be more in control of your feelings than the average person, because you have to help others with their feelings. I find myself continually trying to reassure you that this is not about you. Why is that? How can you possibly support a child or a parent if emotions get in the way? If you let your emotions be in control of your actions, you cannot write an unbiased, professional report on an IEP, can you? Know that I am just a mom who is trying to help her son.

I asked the advocate if they should go to Due Process, but she did not respond. I could not afford it anyway so I tried thinking of ways to put my son in a different school district. Johnie had been in three different schools in this district and the staff appear to be very poorly trained in being able to identify and know how to work with a child who has ASD. Even the Autism Team appears to be very poorly trained and that strikes me as very odd. This is supposed to be a really good school district.

A friend suggested that we move into their neighborhood. They had a good special needs program in their school. When I called their school, the special needs program "was full." It was the same at

every school that I had called. I knew that if he was a neuro-typical child, we could have just enrolled him. A child with an IEP is very difficult to place. I wrote several letters asking for a new IEP meeting and nobody responded. We felt helpless and had no idea of what to do next.

After the IEP meeting, the Autism Team had promised to train the staff at this school to be able to help Johnie with his needs. In about a month, I had asked the SLP on the Team (who is supposed to do the training), when she was going to train the staff and she said she already had. It was quite obvious that did not happen.

A friend of mine took it upon herself to call Johnie's.'s BD teacher and ask if she was trained to work with children who have autism. Sure enough, the teacher admits that she had no qualifications or training in that area of expertise. I reported that to the principal and shortly afterward:..........

Johnie was bullied by one of his teachers and locked in a time-out room for two hours for his reaction to the bullying.

I called the police who told me to call social services.

Social services told me to call district.

District told me to call the principal.

The principal asked me how I knew he was telling the truth.

First of all, there were six witnesses. Some of these had experienced the same treatment. I produced the list of witnesses and some of their home phone numbers.

Secondly, he is generally very honest. He had difficulties telling the story as if it was painful to relive. The teacher saying, "You think your so tough!" was hard for him to talk about. Then, he was pushed into a timeout room where he was banging on the little window in the door over and over again until they put a paper over the window which left him in complete darkness and fear. He tried to minimize the situation by saying that he was grateful that he had his coat with him so that he could sleep comfortably, while he waited for them to let him out.

Somehow, the Autism Team appears to be involved in this situation. After the bullying situation, The SLP from the Autism Team took it upon herself to report the situation. Please note: It is not her place to report situations that are happening in the schools. She does not work there.

Autism Team SLP writes: Johnie will not attend school Wed/Thurs. This week due to anxiety and escalation.

When I asked for a copy of the email she sent out to everybody else but me, she sent out this:

Autism Team SLP writes: Johnie will not attend school Wed/Thurs this week.

I have been very concerned about the qualifications of the Autism Team and now I am concerned about what exactly she feels she needs to hide? Why is she changing the content of the email when she sends me a copy? I must question why she is involved? Why is she reporting this situation? Is the Autism Team trying to create a record of behaviors from Johnie because they can't seem to get enough behaviors naturally to qualify for the SIED label? It all just gets more and more mind boggling every day.

This happened a week before school was out. I pulled him out of the school and brought him back just for his continuation ceremony in which he also received a math award.

Now he is afraid to go into small rooms alone. He is afraid of being locked in.

I could see that the teachers were acting very different toward Johnie since he had received his first IEP. Indeed, they were acting quite different toward me since then too. You can actually see it in the way they communicate on the IEP's. On the first IEP, the teachers had written that Johnie may have been socially awkward, but he was never a behavior problem. They all wrote that he is a very compliant and cooperative child. Now the teachers appear to be trying to create a behaviorally challenged child. Should I presume that is because they put the wrong label on the IEP and did not want to admit the mistake? Who knows. It felt as if Johnie and I were experiencing two different worlds. The uncomfortable world was at school where everyone was acting harsh and saying really creepy things that didn't make sense at all. As soon as we walked out of the school district, we could relax and feel normal. It was the weirdest thing you could possibly imagine.

And so, Johnie and I were always grateful for summer vacation where the worries were forgotten for more than two months of peace.

SIXTH GRADE

The staff provides Johnie and I with a packet of paperwork to show expectations in their SED (Social /Emotional Dysfunction) program for the coming school year.

Aug. 17 – I wrote a letter in response:

1. It looks like a great program for a neuro-typical child with behavioral problems.

2. This program would have to be modified to work for a child with Asperger's Syndrome.

3. Conduct cards and points sheets need to be written with more clarity. Example: The statement "Turning things around", can be very confusing to a child with AS who thinks literally.

4. Johnie should not be anywhere close to children with behavioral problems. They cause unnecessary stress and can easily manipulate the very naive child with AS, into doing things they should not.

5. Johnie needs continual reassurance and explanations.

6. Unstructured time periods can be extremely overwhelming and needs to be monitored or modified.

7. AS children are typically very disorganized and Johnie will need assistance in understanding how he can be more organized rather than getting in trouble for his organization difficulties.

8. What about sensory difficulties? Are you going to understand that he needs breaks occasionally in a quiet or safe haven?

9. What if he is unable to complete the work in class because he is unable to understand, unable to concentrate, or unable to write that fast?

10. Would it be a disruption in class if he were doing his run-around? Why?

11. What if Johnie does not realize his language is inappropriate?

I am sorry that we can not sign your paperwork. It is not appropriate for the needs of children with AS and clearly, inappropriate for the needs of Johnie.

Johnie usually starts every school year feeling sure of himself and his capabilities. He has had two months to build his self-esteem and his self confidence. By the time school lets out, well, maybe this will give you the feeling of what it has been like for him. The blue numbers refer back to the letter that I wrote explaining the boys needs before school started.

Sept 1 - Uncomfortable on special needs bus. (5)

- Uncomfortable with a teachers introduction speech. (5)

- Lost points sheet. (7)

Sept. 3 - Johnie receives a positive referral award for helping a girl open her locker.

- Parent note - this gives high hopes that the school is more focused on the positive. Yeah!

Sept. 5 - Johnie did not understand why he got in trouble for laughing and the other boy did not get in trouble at all. (5,4)

Sept. 28 - Avoids large crowds on the stairs. (5,6)

Oct. 2 - Johnie threw a pencil in class because another boy made him do it. (4)

Oct. 2 - Computer discipline alert - Johnie uses poor language. (4)

    - Parent note - Johnie is afraid of people who use poor language.

    - Unless Johnie did not realize what he was saying, this wasn't him. (11)

Oct. 12 - Learning bully-proofing but unable to understand how to use it. (5)

    - I took Johnie to the social worker to explain more details. (5)

    - What if he does not know the name? Who does he tell? What if the bully gets mad? etc...(5)

    - Johnie is eating lunch and wants to make a friend, so he gave a kid part of his lunch.
      Three days later, he doesn't want to come home hungry every day, but does not want to
      loose a friend either. What does he do? (5)

Oct. 13 - Johnie is having constant problems in the SED classroom. (4,5)

    - He lost his ID. (7)

    - Johnie is terrified of getting in trouble. (5)

    - Johnie gets work for the week to do at home and a meeting is set up to get him out of the
      SED class. It is obvious he is having no behavioral difficulties in his other classes. (4)

10-16- Dear Director:

    I find it kind of funny that you would feel it was appropriate to announce that I was stressed at our meeting. Why would I be stressed? My son is special needs and your school district has placed him in very inappropriate settings for many years now. Why should I be stressed? We have no choice. We must worry. You have given us that. Show me that I have no reason to be stressed and I will show you that I am not.

Oct. 17 - Johnie asked a teacher to write a note promising that he would be put into a better
      classroom. Why? In fourth grade, many promises were made that were never met. (5)

Oct. 19 – Johnie is confused in Science class. (3,5)

    - Johnie is unable to take notes. (5,9)

    - He does not see point of the class if he is just going to get an F for not understanding,
      disorganization, etc. (3,7,9)

- Science happens to be a favorite subject of his.

Oct. 26 – He lost his homework. (7)

Dec. 8 - Four people from the Autism Team come to interview the boy. Very stressful. No warning. All strangers. Johnie said to say sorry to them. He may not have answered the questions correctly.

(2,3,5)

Dec. 11 - Johnie is confused with the schedule change. (5)

    - He is unable to comprehend work in science class. (3,5,9)

    - Unable to comprehend same work in tutorials. (3,5,9)

    - Working in a group made it impossible. (3,5,6,9)

    - That night, it took five minutes to show him how to do the work and another ten minutes for him to complete the work. (5,8)

Dec. 15 - Johnie lost homework - confusion. (7)

    - Teacher worried about Johnie sitting there doing nothing. (3,5,7,9,10)

    - Two teachers assuming Johnie is avoiding the work when his capabilities show the exact opposite. (9)

    - Johnie is moved to a different table. Stressful. No clarification. (5)

Dec. 18 - Trouble with another child was so stressful that Johnie is afraid to go to school. (5)

Jan. 4 - Johnie has assigned seating next to another boy in three classes who throws rocks at him and others. (4,5,6,9)

Jan. 7 - The principal allows Johnie to do on-line courses for some of his classes. (5,6,7,9)

Jan. 23 – Johnie walked out of class. Too much commotion. (5,8,9)

Feb. 6 - Johnie and I were sitting in the office talking over the latest stress. A very nice couple sat down with us for a bit. They have a daughter with Asperger's too. They are there to register her for next year. A teacher came up to them and spoke to them for a bit about the autism program that she was in charge of in this school. Johnie and I looked at each other in astonishment. We realized that he also had a diagnosis of Aspergers and had never met this woman. This left us with an odd an unsettling feeling, so we both got up and quietly left the school. (2,5)

- Johnie and I set up an impromptu meeting several days later with several staff members to explain the stresses and to ask about the mysterious teacher. Every one of them were talking in circles, being evasive, and generally avoiding communication. It was really creepy. (2,3,5)

Mar. 17 – Johnie wrote an incident report: Someone punched me, then another guy punched me..(5,6)

Mar. 23 - Johnie is afraid of a teacher. (5)

- She is mean and won't answer when he asks a question. (5)
- Johnie knows the staff will not understand if he tells them this, so he "made up" an excuse for not attending that class. (5,8)

Mar. 25 - The social worker suggests that Johnie needs to be assertive. (5)

- Johnie replied "Being assertive with peers is like hitting the tail on the donkey. Being assertive with teachers is like trying to block a crocodile attack."

   - Somehow he has no problem being assertive with friends and family.

April 6 - A teacher is shadowing Johnie in his core classes and making him feel uncomfortable. ((5)

   - Johnie is stressed by a threat of a referral for drumming his pencil on the table. (5)

   - Johnie is stressed because the staff won't let him call me. (5)

April 18 - Johnie keeps trying to bring up the autism program and the teacher he has never met.
      This time he goes to the assistant principal who takes Johnie and I to a room for
      severely autistic children. Obviously he is trying to hide something from us. Stress. (5)

April 23 - I spent the day observing Johnie at school to see what the difficulties are.

   - I observed three teachers in one classroom avoiding helping or even talking to Johnie. (5)

   - I could literally see my son being unable to function with doing simple math because

   - of the commotion in the room. (8)

   - The staff is clearly not trained to know how to work with kids who have a neurological
      disorder.

May 3 – The principal of the school blew up at me right in front of Johnie for not trusting her staff to
      care for him. Stress.

   - I wrote to the assistant principal to explain. This is all very excruciating, frustrating, and
      uncomfortable for us all. Johnie suffers the most. He lives it every day. I know you are all
      professionals but, metaphorically speaking, I am really tired of leaving my son with the
      dentist when he should be seeing the doctor. The principal is angry at the wrong person.

May 21 - Johnie and I receive a letter from an attorney threatening truancy court. Stress.

   - Johnie got so worried that he tried going back to school, but called me by noon.

   - I tried to call the attorney on numerous occasions. As I explained to the principal,
      I can't wait to tell the judge what is happening here.

   - Unfortunately, the letter appeared to be only a threat. Nobody responded, no one answered.

Johnie spent most of second semester at home. Although he tried many times to go back to school, it
was a constant nightmare that would not end. Two teachers gave him homework every week that he
completed and returned for more. The rest of his classes he did on-line. It was sad. He did not want to
be left all alone at home.

SIXTH GRADE IEP

Sept 30 – I sent an e-mail to a person on the Autism Team to explain that Johnie's needs have not been met and that he should not be in the SED (Serious Emotional Disability) program.

That person writes: "We serve students by need, not by diagnostics."

Dec. 18 - The same person proved that to be a false statement by listing all Johnie's diagnostics onto the new IEP.

I wrote a letter. If the diagnostics are going to be listed on the IEP, they also need to list all the discrepancies that have caused the misdiagnosis, and I listed them point, by point, by point.

DIDN'T HAPPEN.

I wrote several more letters explaining why Johnie should not be in the SED program and why he does not fit the criteria for the SED label on the IEP.

I also did a survey of fifty friends asking if they had ever seen behavioral problems from Johnie. Not one of them had ever witnessed seeing him with any behavioral problems. He is generally very quiet and well mannered.

NO RESPONSE.

Jan. 15 - Second meeting for the IEP.

A teacher came to the meeting and explained that Johnie has expressed "autistic and GT tendencies." District administration was present at that meeting and told the teacher that he could not acknowledge the obvious even though she had a copy of the diagnosis done by the specialist, even though I showed her that his first and second grade teachers have acknowledged the obvious, and even though I have shown her the obvious.

To teacher: I was surprised to hear you compare Johnie to autistic characteristics.

Teacher: I said that he exhibits both autistic and GT tendencies. Those comments are based on classroom and hallway observations. I have had autistic students in my classroom before.

WHAT?

I kept insisting that Johnie does not fit the criteria for an SED label on the IEP. He also fits all the criteria for autism.

Nope. They kept insisting that he does not. Even with all the evidence they had, they wouldn't budge.

Well, I pointed out, "He is obviously special needs and obviously not SED. What label does he fit, SLD (Speech/language disability)?"

Another meeting was set up to discuss the label on the IEP.

Jan. 27 - An "expert" was brought in to explain why the boy would not fit the label of SLD. (Ironically, this label was put on the Johnie's IEP three years later)

End of discussion. Johnie gets an SED label.

Mom sent out an e-mail after that meeting to ask: "Why is it OK to fudge the facts on an SED label but not on an SLD label?"

The advocate asks: "Please explain how you see facts are being 'fudged'."

Mom replies: "Johnie does not have behavioral problems outside of school. He does not have social/emotional dysfunction unless he is around the same. This is within normal developmental expectations for a child on the autism spectrum who has not been taught how to cope in these situations appropriately for his condition. Johnie cannot have the SED label because he does not fit the criteria.

NO RESPONSE.

THE "INDEPENDENT" DIAGNOSTIC EVALUATION

I asks district to pay for an independent diagnostic evaluation.

District agrees to pay for it and provided me with three numbers to choose from.

I quickly realizes that two of the numbers were not legitimate (One was a brain injury specialist and the other was a junior partner who was not qualified to take on our case). I asked for two more numbers of legitimate independent evaluators.

REQUEST DENIED.

I began to wonder if this was an "independent" evaluation. I had been cautioned by other families that the independent evaluations paid for by district, are paid to diagnose in their favor. Johnie had missed so much school already and neither of us wanted him to miss any more. The whole process is taking so long and we wanted him back in school as soon as possible. What choice did we have? I had to trust. I had to move forward and accept the situation as it was. Big mistake.

Four months later, we are back to creepier than ever:

PDD NOS

Anxiety Disorder

Presence of unusual and illogical thinking

Auditory Processing Disorder

Disorder of Written Expression

This diagnosis is clearly written for the benefit of the district and does not have a thing to do with the child's needs.

Doctor: "Johnie has a confusing diagnostic history."

Parent comment: I showed this doctor why Johnie's history is not confusing at all. She had all the documentation to show what happened to him and why the misdiagnosis is common with kids who have mild autism. This doctor should not have been confused at all.

British Journal of Psychiatry: "The similarity of Asperger's Syndrome to a preschizophrenic, schizoid personality disorder as well as to residual schizophrenia, in both clinical presentation and neurobiology, has led to a diagnostic confusion that has not taken into account their differing developmental trajectories."

Note: This article was sent with the last diagnosis of psychosis because I had asked the doctor to send proof that the boys run-around was a sign of psychosis.

'Psychosis in Childhood and its Management' by Paramjit T. Joshi and Kenneth E. Towbin: Children routinely have intrusions of fantasy into ordinary mental life. They have not developed the cognitive abilities that permit them to observe and compare their experiences in an objective manner.

Disorganized speech is an inherent component of many of the developmental disorders (like Asperger's Syndrome). Clearly, the assessment and ascertainment of delusions, hallucinations, and thought disorder in linguistically impaired children are difficult and complicated.

Doctor: "A school observation was not included as part of this evaluation."

Parent comment: I would think this would be extremely important to discern WHY Johnie is so stressed at school and not in his personal life. This doctor should know better.

The Colorado Resource Guide for Autism Spectrum Disorders: "A brief observation in a single setting cannot present a true picture of a individuals abilities or behavior patterns."

Doctor: "Given Johnie's anxiety symptoms and the extent to which they interfere with his functioning in the school setting, Cognitive-Behavioral Therapy is recommended. CBT at _____Medical Center is recommended."

Parent comment: I took Johnie to only two therapy appointments because it became immediately obvious that he cannot generalize his knowledge. As a doctor who specializes in ASD, she should have known that Johnie is expected to have anxiety at school and should be getting CBT on location because of his inability to generalize his knowledge. Either she is not a specialist or she is trying to create a false report.

Elly Tucker: "They do not automatically know how to generalize what they learn to new situations."

Temple Grandin: "If he is taught in only one location, the child will think that the rule only applies to one specific place."

Michael D. Powers: "He'll also have trouble generalizing skills that he's learned at home, or in small group settings, to the classroom."

Tony Attwood: One of the issues during the practice stage of CBT will be generalization. People with Asperger's Syndrome tend to be quite rigid in terms of recognizing when the new strategies are applicable in a situation that does not obviously resemble the practice sessions.

Doctor: (Phone conversations with school personnel) "Johnie has said that 'the voices tell me to do something', and has stated that thoughts are confusing and at times controlling him"

Parent comment: First of all, there is no record of Johnie talking that way in school. There is only a record of him not understanding the leading questions of the doctors at the hospital when he was in third grade. Since this is written in the present context, district administration who had hired her, were the only ones who could have told the doctor to write this on the diagnosis even though it is not true. WHY? Again, it is quite obvious that this doctor is trying to create a false diagnostic report on Johnie.

Tony Attwood: "Another problem with the pragmatic and semantic aspects of language that occurs with people who have AS, is that they often make a literal interpretation of a question. A psychiatrist may ask a question such as "Do you hear voices?" A person with AS would answer the question correctly as "Yes." They literally hear voices of people talking around them all day."

Doctor: "Although there was no evidence of florid psychotic symptoms during the current evaluations, Johnie does continue to display unusual and illogical thinking that is not entirely consistent with an autism spectrum diagnosis."

Parent comment: The only time I have seen any evidence of unusual or illogical communication (I say that because this doctor has no idea how a person is thinking), is when Johnie has been with doctors. Usually he is incredibly logical and cannot understand when others are not. Again it is the very nature in which she writes this report that conveys a creepiness that is virtually dripping with unprofessional and tabloid style reporting.

Temple Grandin: "Children and adults on the autism spectrum are concrete, literal thinkers. Ideas that cannot be understood through logic or that involve emotions and social relationships are difficult for us to grasp, and even more difficult to incorporate into our daily lives."

Tony Attwood: "In my opinion, unusual language abilities are an essential characteristic of Asperger's Syndrome and should be included in future revisions of the DSM criteria."

Doctor: "I asked Johnie to respond to a series of picture cards. He generally told brief stories that required some prompting on my part in order to tell a complete story. He displayed somewhat unusual perceptions about what was happening in the pictures. The story line of his responses was at times hard to follow and illogical; i.e. when talking about a lost boy, he said that the boy could tell which way the wind was blowing 'by the way his hair was blowing', or in another story the man 'accidentally ate his credit card because he was eating spaghetti and his credit card was in the spaghetti.' in another story card, a boy is holding a chair as if he is going to throw it; the boy tells the story that the boy in the story is mad at the chair, because it is a 'magical chair' and the chair hit him."

Parent comment: Please note that this doctor is using these cards in an inappropriate fashion. Does she actually not know how to use them or was she trying to show something that really is not there?

Instead of showing Johnie's poor problem solving skills as these cards are intended, she is using his naivete to show something illogical. Please read on to see how a professional uses them.

Specialist diagnostic report (on Johnie the previous year - and rejected by district), using the same picture cards: Johnie was shown problem solving pictures, asked to describe the problem and explain what could be done to solve the problem. He is able to describe and explain simple pictures, for example, a little girl who could not reach a water fountain or a ladder that broke to a tree house. But when shown a picture of a birds nest that had fallen on the ground, children looking at it, a mother bird hovering above, and a cat about to pounce, the boy stated 'the chicks just hatched and their sad, this bird is trying to eat the chicks.' Johnie completely missed the problem and therefore the solution. The more involved the problem, as far as complexity and amount, the more difficult it was for him to understand the problems and therefore the solution.

This doctor is well aware of the anxiety symptoms experienced by youth on the autism spectrum because she has presented training opportunities about her ongoing clinical research in that area. Still, she writes: "Anxiety Disorder NOS."

Parent comment: I have gone out of my way to show that Johnie has the potential for anxiety but we help him through it. I even provided the doctor with a survey I have done on him, and she wrote:

Doctor: "None of them indicated that Johnie displayed significant difficulties."

Parent comment: Why is she accentuating anxiety when it is only problematic in the schools? Again it appears to be a report that is created to protect the school district from the mistakes they have made in the care of my son. Johnie would not have the degree of anxiety that he has at school if he was properly cared for.

Tony Attwood: "Many children and adults with Asperger's Syndrome appear to be prone to being anxious for much of their day.

Parent comment: I have also shown documentation to this doctor and the district that anxiety is created because he is inappropriately placed.

The Autism Team wrote: Amidst considerable stresses including a sense of fear of being bullied by peers, concerns about interpersonal rejection by peers,etc..

Parent comment: Knowing that Johnie is stressed by the bullies, The Autism Team recommends he remain in a classroom full of bullies namely BD/SED (Behavioral Disorder/ Serious Emotional Disorder) classrooms? How does that make sense?

Tony Attwood: "I have noted the frequent bullying of children with Asperger's Syndrome, has led to their being referred for the treatment of clinical depression. Sometimes, when the repeated requests by the child with Asperger's Syndrome for the bullying to stop have failed, as have ignoring the bullying or reporting it to an adult, the degree of depression experienced by the child is such that he feels there is no other option but suicide.

Temple Grandin: The children's rhyme says, "Sticks and stones will break your bones but words will never hurt you." It's not true; words hurt a lot.

The teachers guide I had passed out to all of Johnie's teachers by Karen Williams: "Protect the child from bullying and teasing."

Your little professor.com and other sources:

- It would be ideal to make sure that kids with AS are in a smaller class size so they will experience less distractions and more individual attention.
- Unfortunately, some school districts do not feel they can afford this unless the AS child is placed in an SED program.
- Although AS kids tend to react to their environment in such a way as to be labeled "behavioral", they should never, ever be placed into a BD or SED program or classroom.
- In an SED program, kids with AS will not be learning the social skills they need. STRESS
- They will not understand the behavioral lessons in this program. STRESS
- The sensory stimulation in these programs are far more intense and generally far more aggravating to the child who has AS. STRESS
- Their peers will be far less intelligent and less inclined to want to learn. This in turn is why the curriculum is modified which is inappropriate for the AS child who's IQ is average to above average. STRESS
- Their peers in this program will be more "streetwise" than the AS child and he will inevitably, be easily bullied. STRESS
- The teachers have to be more firm with the children in this program which can be quite a bit more frightening to the child with AS who does not usually understand. STRESS

Parent comment: Why isn't the doctor indicating that placement in the school could be a very real factor in creating the stress? She had all the documentation that I provided for her and she has the training as a specialist to know better.

Clearly, this diagnosis was written for the benefit of the district. Although she wrote PDD NOS on the diagnosis to indicate that Johnie clearly has all the characteristics of a child with high functioning autism, she couldn't indicate the obvious Asperger's Syndrome because she was hired to show the confusion that district has. We have to speculate how this is ethical?

The district did agree to pay for appropriate social skills classes for Johnie that summer which he had never had before, so we were very grateful for that.

SEVENTH GRADE

Negotiations with district led to Johnie being placed in yet another school. The poor kid had now been in a different school every year since third grade to avoid the commotion.

The school was small with smaller class sizes and a separate wing for the autistic kids. This was certainly what he needed. The creepy part was that unfortunately, it was an SED school. I was again, quite horrified. How is Johnie (who is gifted), going to learn anything in an SED school? That is the most ridiculous thing ever! You cannot put autistic kids in an SED school and expect it to work. Anyone who specializes in ASD would know better. The fact that this school exists, shows that this district knows nothing about ASD!

However, the advocate insisted that the staff at the school was very good. All that Johnie and I could do was accept the situation. It did not appear as if there were any options. None were given.

Johnie started seventh grade with the same self-confidence that he usually did after a summer of freedom from the confusion. Again, he tried so hard to be social, to fit in, to be accepted. Again, he fails. This time he got in trouble for trying to help the teachers learn how to work with the autistic boys. Again, he has no idea why he got in trouble. He was just trying to be helpful.

I started the school year with quite a different experience than I had ever felt since Johnie had received his first IEP. It was really weird. Staffing, particularly the social worker, appeared to want to know

Johnie's needs. The social worker was receptive to hearing why he should not be in this school, why he

did not survive sixth grade, why he is and always has had ASD and never had any signs of psychosis. It was such a relief to me to finally be able to unburden myself of all that I knew and all that Johnie and I had gone through in this school district.

I explained to the social worker that Johnie and I had never in our lives, ever experienced so much discomfort, so much anger and dissension, than we had experienced in these schools. It is like

living in two different worlds. The nightmare is here in this district and the joy we experience in life is everywhere else. That is why I told him, "What is happening to us in these schools, does not have a thing to do with the two of us."

I spoke about writing hundreds of letters over the years because nobody was listening when I tried to tell them Johnie's needs. Sometimes they would get angry as if I was telling them how to do their job, when I was just trying to tell them that Johnie should not be in their classroom. My focus has always been Johnie's needs, not them. I am his mother after all, and I know him better than anyone. The social worker seemed to be interested in those letters, so I brought them to school for him to read.

The social worker spoke of wanting to set up a meeting with staff to give the feeling of autism. He wondered if I had any ideas. I had a stockpile of ideas because of a dream of making a film one day, and I shared my ideas with him. He eventually had his meeting and told me that he had used many of my ideas and they had worked quite well.

FEELING A BIT AUTISTIC -WORKSHOP

Let us set up a workshop where we are gathering to try to get a feel of what is is like for these kids who have high functioning autism. Temple Grandin points out that "neurotypical people have a lot of difficulty imagining how debilitating sensory issues can be." So, we need to set up the room to give that feeling.

- Prepare coffee for everyone that is brewed much too strong.
- Have cookies on the table that have been baked with too much salt in them.
- Place a bowl of apples and oranges on the table that have all been injected with lemon juice.
- Have the radio blasting some music into the room.
- Loosen a light bulb, so that it flickers.
- Have the table covered with a wool cloth that has salt sprinkled all over it.

Exorcise #1: All participants are required to participate in this exorcise with an agreed upon action of irritation (kick the table leg, whisper to your neighbor and point to random people, tap your pencil, etc.). They are also required to fill out a worksheet entirely with the hand they do not normally use. This is to give the feeling of poor motor coordination. These kids often struggle with literal thinking and so each participant is required to try to think literally about filling out the worksheet. For example: What do you do if your sentence or word does not fit on the line? Try to come up with as many literal interpretations as possible throughout the workshop.

Autism is a neurological disorder. To describe it in the simplest of forms, dysfunctions in the neural structures of the amygdala, hippocampus, septum, mammillary bodies and the cerebellum have been identified. These affect planning and control, emotional regulation, and motor coordination.

Exorcise #2: To get a feeling for it, let us start with the motor coordination: Pick up a pencil and write the sentence above with the hand you do not normally use. You will find that it is difficult. Pay attention to your concentration level. Do you find that you are so busy concentrating on the writing, that you are having a more difficult time paying attention to what is happening around you?

Exorcise #3: Let's try restricted interest: Imagine that it is very difficult to attend to more than one thing at a time. You love trains. You research them often. Someone yells at you "DO NOT THINK ABOUT TRAINS. IT IS VERY IMPORTANT THAT YOU ERASE THE THOUGHT OF TRAINS, TRAIN TRACKS, TRAIN DISPATCHER, TRAINLOAD, OR TRAINING FROM YOUR MIND."

OK, now let us remember: "It is often difficult to concentrate while keeping eye contact with whom you are conversing."

What are you thinking about?

Exorcise #4: Using that restricted interest, lets try a concentration test. Make sure all participants weed out the commotion and rewrite the list as it is being read to them (no peeking). Also make sure you are using the hand that you do not normally use.

1. Put your train track shoes in the train track closet.
2. Clean the train dishes and train dispatcher dry them.
3. Put your train coat in your trainload room.
4. Make your pokemon lunch with pokemon sausage and pokemon milk.
5. Do pages pokemon 426-428 in the pokemon algebra book.

Although children with high functioning autism usually speak fluently, they generally do not comprehend what you mean without support.

Exorcise #5: THE PET ANALOGY

Imagine you are training your puppy to go potty outside. You leave for a couple of hours and the puppy has an accident while you are gone. When you return, you know you cannot get mad at the puppy and point to the puddle expecting them to comprehend. They do not speak our language. While it remains obvious that you are angry about the puddle, what are you expecting from him?? If you catch him in the act and put him outside a few times, he will eventually understand.

* It is virtually the same for a child with high functioning autism. Although they speak the language, they will not comprehend unless you catch them in the moment and explain your expectations very clearly and succinctly.

I have taught my parakeet to speak our language, but I never expected her to comprehend the meaning. That part of the brain that helps the average person intuitively comprehend a situation based upon their past experiences, does not function properly in autistic children. They do not understand how to generalize their experiences from one situation to the next.

- If you can see that the boy is speaking fluently, (just as my parakeet does), would you expect the boy to understand? Why or why not???

Exorcise #6: Children with high functioning autism will often perceive things entirely differently than we imagine. Let's give an example of conflicting perceptions. "Who's on First" by Abbott & Costello.

Costello: What's the guys name on first base?

Abbott: No. What is on second.

Costello: I'm not asking you who's on second.

Abbott: Who's on first.

Costello: I don't know.

Abbott: He's on third, we're not talking about him.

Costello: Now how did I get on third base?

Abbott: Why you mentioned his name.

Costello: If I mentioned the third baseman's name, who did I say is playing third?

Abbott: No. Who's playing first.

Costello: What's on first?

Abbott: What's on second.

Costello: I don't know.

Abbott: He's on third.

Costello: There I go, back on third again!

Example A: A boy with autism was asked what he thought of his one month old niece. He said, "She's lazy." Why does he have that perception? What perception is he missing? What does he need to learn?

Example B: An autistic boy is asked to show the front of his book. He fiddles with his book, obviously in deep concentration as his tongue is sticking out a little bit. He turns the book this way and that way until finally, he proudly shows you the paper edge of the book. Why? Thinking logically, why would he show you the paper edge? What was his perception? What does he need to learn from this situation?

Example C: An autistic boy comes up to you and he tells you that he hurt his finger real bad. He said he stuck his finger in paint and it hurt bad. Yes, this is a true story and he was speaking honestly. Thinking literally, what would he mean? (Answer: He was running down the stairs and jammed his finger in the wall, which was covered with paint). How do you get the correct interpretation of the situation from him? What does he need to learn from this situation?

Exorcise #7: If we understand that these children will have difficulties with multi-tasking or being able to concentrate on a list of tasks, how do we teach them how to ride a bike? It took me four years to realize that my son needed to learn one step at a time. I bought him heelies (shoes with wheels on the heels), so that I could teach him how to balance on the wheels, how to role on the wheels, and then how to steer. A good friend suggested that this can easily be done by just taking the pedals of the bike for a while. It is important to teach "The parts before the whole" to these children. How would you teach them about the universe? Would you teach it different than you do now?

Exorcise #8: Now, lets pay close attention to all of your senses. What do you smell in the room? Name the different smells. What smells make you uncomfortable? Why? When you shut down one sensory perception, the others become more noticeable and clear. If you are struggling with this exorcise, close your eyes a minute and pay close attention to everything that you feel around you. What does the air feel like? Is your clothing comfortable? What about taste? Visual? What is audible to you in the room? Does it make concentration difficult? Why? What sounds are comforting? What sounds are uncomfortable to you?

Exorcise #9: As you are taking the time to pay attention to your senses, do you find yourself getting more and more uncomfortable. Imagine being a child who does not know how to explain feelings, and these kids really don't until they are taught. Can you see why they would want to run from this situation? Not knowing how to explain in a way you would understand, can you feel why they would want to react, like yelling, or screaming? Can you feel the tension building higher and higher, the longer you remain in the room? Can you feel the need for a jog, a need to stretch, or attend to something much more relaxing? Can you imagine why the pacing and hand flapping is so vitally important to them? It is all so utterly overwhelming to them at times, that they really need space to catch up and refocus, because the really do not know how else to relieve the Brain Zinnie.

FEELING A BIT AUTISTIC - WORKSHEET

Directions: Please do not fill out this worksheet unless you are writing with the hand you do not normally use.

Exorcise #1 Literal thinking: What do you do if your sentence or word does not fit on the line?

_____

_____

Exorcise #2 Motor Coordination: _____

_____

_____

Exorcise #3 Restricted interest: What does this exorcise cause you to think about? Why? _____

_____

Exorcise #4 Focus: 1._____

2._____   3._____

4._____   5._____

Exorcise #5 Comprehension: If you see that the boy is speaking fluently, would you expect the boy to understand? Why or why not?_____

_____

_____

Exorcise #6 Perceptions:
    Example A) Why does he have that perception? What perception is missing? What does he need to learn?_____

_____

Example B) Why? Thinking logically, why would he show you the paper edge? What was his perception? What does he need to learn?_____

Example C) How did you get the correct interpretation of this situation from him? What is the lesson here?_____

Exorcise #7 Multitasking: How do you teach multitasking? How would you teach the universe?
_____
_____

Exorcise #8 Sensory: Identify all of your sensory perceptions.
TASTE_____

TOUCH_____

SMELL_____

SIGHT_____

HEAR_____

Exorcise #9 Feelings/Emotions/Reaction: Explain how you are feeling right now while attending this workshop. _____
_____
_____

Are you feeling sympathetic to people with high functioning autism? _____
_____

Define: Brain zinnie_____

These conversations helped relieve the stress that I had not even realized I had been carrying around with me. The burden of it all was slowly lifted as the social worker and I were able to laugh and joke around while discussing Johnie's needs.

On day while I was speaking to the social worker, I told him a story: "One of the other mothers was telling us why she was very angry at you. I told her that she should not be angry at you because you are just a peon in the system that does not work very well."

Social worker: "Peon? You think I'm a peon?"

Mom: "No, I never said that you specifically were a peon. We are all, each and every one of us a peon in the system."

For some reason, he wouldn't let go of the word (even a year later), and I thought that was very strange. Why would he take a word completely out of context of the story? Was he showing his insecurities? Maybe he was told to turn off the charm? Oh, who knows. Since he had listened to all kinds of harsh realities that I had presented without batting an eye, and even added stories of his own for many months, I had to surmise that something was amiss. The conversations were never quite the same after that but I thanked him for helping me let go of the stress.

By January, Johnie was getting phone numbers from some of his new friends and all the parents rallied together to form a support group. This was great for Johnie because now he had friends "like him" and he didn't feel so alone with his odd characteristics.

I had other parents to talk to who had all gone through similar difficulties in the schools. I also, did not feel so alone as I had for so many years. We all shared our knowledge and research and most of all, we could all laugh and joke around about the oddities that we must accept on a daily basis, just because we have kids with high functioning autism. So. four families got together once a month and it was really wonderful for us all to have that connection.

While it appears as if my needs are being met to some degree, Johnie's needs are still not being met at school. Even though they are acknowledging his autism, it still appears as if staff are working with an SED kid. So, I go back to writing many letters.

I explained to the social worker that Johnie has been tested as gifted and that he has always done quite well in math. What is happening in math class this year does not make any sense at all. In a mainstream classroom (last year), I showed him that Johnie was able to get 37 assignments done in a month and still had a grade of A-. This year (in an SED classroom), Johnie is expected to only get 16 assignments done in one month, and his grade is a C-. Explain how that could possibly be?

Math teacher: The changes I have seen have been mostly him having more difficulty staying focused. Even with a conversation with me, he tends to lose his thought and stop, close his eyes, and then really think about what he was trying to communicate. His grade has dropped in math because of this lack of focus. He currently sits at a "C".

Parent comment: If this teacher has not noticed his difficulties in focusing on task till now (December), he is not paying attention. Please notice that the teacher is grading Johnie on his disability, rather than abilities in math.

Teacher: The students were talking yesterday about how they are getting annoyed at Johnie for copying them even after they ask him to stop. He was also humming and making comments to students after he was asked to stop. I do not know if he is intentionally trying to make others mad/annoyed or if he is trying to do what he thinks he should to fit in. I do know that he does not take responsibility for this type of behavior.

Parent comment: Autism is a developmental disability significantly affecting verbal and non verbal communication and social interaction, generally evident before age three that adversely affects a child's educational performance......... Why does this teacher have no idea WHY Johnie is having social difficulties? WHY is she expecting Johnie to take responsibility for something he does not understand? Isn't she supposed to be teaching social skills?

TEACCH autism guide: Usually when persons with high functioning autism become upset or engaged in inappropriate behaviors, they are unlikely to have the skills to appreciate why what they are doing is wrong because they can not form those cause and affect social connections.

Teacher: Johnie has formed a friendship with another boy and he is resistant to feedback about how he is trying to maintain the friendship. In a way he is trying to almost become the other student by copying his mannerisms, etc... sitting next to the student every chance he gets (even after the student states that he needs some space). I am putting a new goal on his points sheet that reads: "Honor the needs and wants of others to develop and maintain healthy friendships."

Parent comment: OK, we are getting really creepy now. Johnie has no desire to BECOME anyone. So, I write to the teacher:

A) The boy and his friend have a very good and healthy friendship outside the school. They get together most weekends and hang for hours and hours with little difficulties.

B) The severe stress in your school causes his friend to feel like being left alone. He does not know how to deal with the stress and should not be expected to, he has AS.

C) The severe stress in your school causes Johnie to want to cling to his friend. He does not know how to deal with the stress and should not be expected to, he has AS.

D) If you put a new goal on his points sheet, you are totally missing the "point". Johnie's friend and that friends mother will both admit to you that the friend is just as much a part of the problem as Johnie is.

E) Johnie and his friend are EQUALLY stressed in your school and are handling the stress in opposite forms. They are not equipped to understand how to handle the stress because they both have AS.

Parent comment (to Social worker): It is very weird that Johnie has so many more behavioral problems at school than anywhere else. It is EXTREMELY hard to grasp that it would be him everyone is describing, day after day. You are the professionals. OK, what is it then?

Social worker: The reason you do not see it is that home life is less demanding and less stressful.

I knew with assurance that the problem was far beyond this simple perception. This teacher and social worker are trying to describe my son as having behavioral problems, when he doesn't. Going back to the first IEP, let's not forget what the staff were saying about my son. "While Johnie may have been socially awkward at school, he was never a behavior problem. He is a very compliant and cooperative child." I wrote many letters and spoke in person with the social worker explaining: "Your opinion means a lot to me. You know that. You describe a relationship between Johnie and his friend in which Johnie copies everything his friend does and even appears to want to be more like his friend. Strangely, we all see a very different picture outside the school. Johnie is so proud of himself and so full of himself, that he lectures to people about what he knows every day. I have even heard him lecture to his friend on several occasions and his friend responds by saying "I'm not stupid.""

The social worker would not listen to me and kept insisting that Johnie had severe and lasting problems that would affect his future relationships. I was forced to assume that the social worker was talking about himself. I had to. After all, he did appear to be a bit insecure about the word "peon". It was too horrible to imagine that this very kind man would willingly admit that the staff was purposefully bullying my son. He was announcing it as if it was no big deal. The teacher had indicated punishing my son for not understanding social skills, and the social worker indicated no help for him at all. It appeared to me as if staff is trying to create a kid to match the label on the first IEP, rather than trying to work with the actual kid.

Johnie was embarrassed to have me around at school because he wanted to be more independence, but he did not know how to explain how bad it was at that school. He asked me to please come shadow him for a day so I could see for myself. What I saw, was horrifying. There was so much commotion of peers talking and cussing and not paying attention to the lesson. There was no room for learning for anyone in most of the classrooms. I pulled Johnie out of school for the last month (as did many other families). We collected homework once a week and Johnie completed it for the next week until school was out.

SUMMER

The summer before Johnie started eighth grade, we hung out quite a bit with our new friends. A new family was added to the group as one boy had started school late. We wanted to make sure that the boys got plenty of socialization exposure and the parents were there to help them out with all the difficulties. We got together once a month as a group and gathered in a different place every time. Usually it was loads of fun but one day we decided to get together at the reservoir for a swim and a picnic. The wind picked up so bad that day, that we had to create an indoor party at the last minute.

The district had a summer social program for all the autistic boys and some of them went. It was dubious as to how helpful it was in a social aspect. Johnie made no friends in that group. They did go on many outings and in this aspect he was exposed to many different experiences which he needed.

I met with district personnel to again try to explain that Johnie cannot be in an SED school. It does not help him with his needs academically or socially. He needs to be in an academically stimulating environment and a socially stimulating environment. The staff needs to be trained in knowing the social needs of a child with autism. Despite the fact that Johnie did make friends last year, those friendships would not have survived without the help of the parents. You can easily see by the teacher comments that the friendships were doomed to fall apart at school. The parents on the other hand, have gone out of their way to help the boys understand HOW to maintain the friendships.

IEP

Social worker: Although it was determined that Johnie would benefit from a smaller structured setting to address his needs, he continues to have a difficult time in this setting. Concerns expressed centered around diagnostic labels as they impacted day-to-day programing for him. Specifically around "behavioral" issues that could be attributed to a PDD (Pervasive Development Disorder) diagnosis as opposed to other social/emotional issues. His reactions appeared to be significantly impacted when exposed to the BD population and less structured settings such as his lunch period. Loud and chaotic environments caused more stress and difficulties around managing sensory overloads. During these times we would observe a "shutting down" reaction to these stressors.

Johnie is a creative and imaginative student. His social skills demonstrate his ability to establish and maintain friendships with peers and adults, who he perceives understand his needs and uniqueness.

Parent comment: Having said that Johnie is capable of establishing and maintaining friends in the last year, why does the staff still insist on giving him the SED label which indicates that he is incapable of maintaining friends. Makes no sense.

According to the rules of The Exceptional Children's Education Act (ECEA)
2.08 (5) (b) Criteria for SIGNIFICANT IDENTIFIABLE EMOTIONAL DISABILITY (SIED)
          preventing the child from receiving reasonable education benefit from regular education
          shall include the following characteristics and qualifiers:
2.08 (5) (b) (i) One or both of the following characteristics shall be present:
          (A) ACADEMIC FUNCTIONING: an inability to receive reasonable educational
              benefit from regular education which is not primarily the result of intellectual,
              sensory or other health factors, but due to the identified emotional condition.

Even with the obvious sensory issues that caused Johnie to feel like running from his classrooms all the time, he managed to exceed academically to such a level as to be placed into the Gifted/Talanted program and still the staff feels he fits into this category. WHY?

2.08 (5) (b) (i) (B) Social/emotional functioning: an inability to build or maintain interpersonal
          relationships which significantly interferes with the childs social development.
          Social development involves those adaptive behaviors and social skills which
          enable a child to meet environmental demands and assume responsibility for
          his/her own and others welfare.

As a child with autism, I could not deny that Johnie did fit into this category as he really had a lot to learn about how to socialize with his peers. He was clearly unable to assume responsibility for his own and others welfare until he learned how.

2.08 (5) (b) (ii) All four of the following qualifiers shall be documented for either of the above characteristics demonstrated.

2.08 (5) (b) (ii) (A) A variety of instructional and/or behavior interventions were implemented within regular education and the child remains unable to receive reasonable education benefit from regular education or his/her presence continues to be detrimental to the education of others.

When Johnie's teachers in first and second grade knew that he had Aspergers, they were able to provide him with an excellent education and help him with most of his academic needs. The only thing during that period that was not attended to was his social needs. Johnie never had any problems learning outside the classroom. He actually has always excelled with anything he put his mind to and enjoyed learning so much that he would often teach us everything he learned. Johnie does not fit into this qualifier because I have provided every school with the teachers guide that his first grade teacher provided to me and none of his teachers used it after his second grade.

2.08 (5) (b) (ii) (B) Indicators of social/emotional dysfunction exist to a marked degree; that is, at a rate and intensity above the child's peers and outside of his/her ethnic and cultural norms and outside the range of normal developmental expectations.

As a child with Aspergers, Johnie is expected to have a social dysfunction. He is even expected to have some emotional dysfunction as he is scrambling to understand everything. Johnie does not fit this qualifier because he has always been inside the range of normal developmental expectations for a child with ASD.

2.08 (5) (b) (ii) (C) Indicators of social/emotional dysfunction are pervasive, and are observable in at least two different settings within the child's environment, one of which shall be the school.

Johnie's social/emotional dysfunction was virtually non-existent outside the schools. Oh yes, he had social difficulties but he was also willing and even enjoyed learning new things as I have said before. Sure he had emotional difficulties once in a while, but he was always willing to learn a new way of responding. He had far less emotional difficulties than an average child. He is normally so well behaved that his presence is often hard to detect. As all the teachers had pointed out in his first IEP, "He is very compliant and cooperative." Johnie has always been cooperative and compliant at home and in the community and therefore does not come close to fitting this qualifier.

2.08 (5) (b) (ii) (D) Indicators of social/emotional dysfunction have existed over a period of time and are not isolated incidents or transient, situational responses to stressors in the child's environment.

Since it is clear that Johnie's social/emotional dysfunctions are isolated to this school district, he does not fit this qualifier. At the time the first IEP was written, Johnie was described by the teachers as cooperative and compliant EXCEPT when he was trying to discuss his feelings (i.e. glitches). That is the "isolated incidents." Johnie does not fit this qualifier.

GOALS on last years IEP:

1. Using proper spacing, capitalization and punctuation for written assignments

2. Cooperatively working with others in group situations when given assignments in classroom situations.

3. When faced with stressful situations in the school environment, Johnie will use strategies to calm himself so that he can return to educational environment.

4. When Johnie makes a negative choice in the school environment, he will be able to verbalize his role and responsibility regarding the situation.

5. Improve Social Language skills by engaging in conversation with another person for appropriate amount of time using greeting, topic of interest, appropriate ending, and taking turns and demonstrating understanding of nonverbal language.

GOALS on this years IEP:

1. Using proper spacing, capitalization and punctuation for written assignments.

2. Johnie will identify and implement strategies to manage his stress and motivate successful performance.

3. Improve Social Language skills by engaging in conversation with another person for appropriate amount of time using greeting, appropriate ending, and taking turns and demonstrating understanding of nonverbal language.

4. Interacting with text by organizing and summarizing information.

5. Using and organizing materials appropriately.

6. Understanding the perceptions of others.

Parent comment: I bring up the goals because they have been virtually ignored for the most part in all these years. EXAMPLE: They had a really good system for teaching the children how to keep their notebooks organized. The problem was, the teacher was working with an SED kid. She showed me how she was working with him. When he did not put a pen in his pencil case, she marked him wrong instead of explaining WHY he needed a pen in his pencil case. This is why he never learned how to be organized. She never kept a daily record of working with his organizational skills. She never sent in quarterly reports as it should be done. Most of his goals in all these years were never recorded. Seeing no improvement, in all these years, I will assume they were often ignored.

Johnie did not want to go back to the same school because it was so horrible and wasn't teaching him a thing. However, they did promise that things would be better and I did not want to send him back to the school he was in for sixth grade because he missed so much school that year. So, he ended up back in the same SED school with a promise of improvements.

EIGHTH GRADE

Mom: Johnie is happy to be in school and happy to be with his friends. He is also worried about two boys showing up, that he is afraid of.

Johnie is also very worried about being challenged appropriately academically, which is the main reason why he wanted to go to the other school.

The vocabulary words are pretty easy for him. Could you test him on the vocabulary words at the beginning of the week so that he does not feel like he is doing things over again?

In math, he learned "place values" about four years ago and "greatest common factor", about two years ago. I am wondering if the teacher could test him and/or ask him what he can do before making him do things he already knows. He does not see the point of doing things over again.

Science was a joy because he was doing things that were new to him.

We are having a food tug-of-war issue at home and it will affect him at school. He might tell you we have no food in our house because that is how it feels to him, but I can assure you that our fridge and cupboards are full. He does qualify for free lunches, so you can ask if he wants one, but he probably won't eat them. He might not bring a lunch and he might not eat at all, but that's OK. I am hoping he will open up to diverse choices as his hunger builds, so please don't make the food issue a big deal.

Mom: (To a teacher) Thank you ever so much for setting up the meeting today. I was glad that Johnie came to advocate for himself. I am sure you realize that the minute you put him to shame, he was unable to advocate for himself anymore. He just shut down. How can we improve this situation?

Teacher: The following is a homework assignment that Johnie did not take home on Thursday. He would not allow me to help him put it in his notebook, and I am not sure if he was simply avoiding or possibly lacking confidence and needs more help.

Mom: Word problems are much more confusing to him than numbers are in math. He did not feel confident that I could show him how to do the work either. This was very hard for him to explain when the bell rang and he had to get to his next class. He has difficulty with multi-tasking.

Teacher: Johnie did not have his binder with him because he refused to put it in his backpack. He told another teacher that he always leaves it here. He also put his science homework in the recycle box, refusing to take it home. The science teacher came and explained the work more thoroughly and he was able to finish it in homeroom. This is the second time he has refused to take homework home.

Mom: Johnie does not know how to multi-task. He is trying to get ready to leave at the same time the new teacher is trying to give him homework he did not remember.

He thought she had given him something by mistake that was not his and that is why it went in the recycle bin.

At the same time, he knew he did not need his binder because he knew he did not have homework.

He was in a rush to leave and it is very hard for him to concentrate and comprehend it all at the same time. He is not trying to avoid homework.

Teacher: Johnie walked out of class without permission of the gym teacher. The para followed Johnie into the hallway, asking him repeatedly to return to the gym, which Johnie refused to do. He was reminded to follow directions so that he could get a cupcake after PE. After PE, most of the students ate cupcakes, while the boy sat outside the room on the bench by the window seat. I tried to talk with him once about why he left the gym without permission, but he would not respond to me. By then he was pretty shut down and upset.

Mom: Johnie was very embarrassed by a situation that had happened in class. He was reaching for a ball between the legs of a friend. The awkward position he got himself into, caused everyone to laugh and caused him to react to a feeling of embarrassment.

Johnie has been running for 8 years and still nobody knows WHY.

Telling him to stop running has never stopped him before or since.

Telling him that it is safer to stay in the classroom IS NOT LOGICAL. He knows it isn't.

Your focus is on the wrong thing.

He will not stop or change "the behavior", until you discover WHY it is happening.

Only then, can you teach him a better way of coping.

Teacher: Today, during a break from testing "his class" went outside for a break -not his ILC (Intensive Learning Center) peers. Several other classes joined in and the teachers structured a kickball game. Johnie was right in the middle of it having a blast, and appeared sad when it was time to stop.

Mom: Johnie did indeed enjoy the kickball, but was kinda sad afterward because he was not doing very well and some of the other players made some rather mean comments about his playing ability. You are aware that he has autism and the other boys do not, right? You are aware that you are "throwing him to the wolves" in a spontaneous game of kickball with a bunch of bullies, right?

Teacher: FYI - As soon as a certain student was off task earlier, so went Johnie......and as soon as a certain student apologized, so did Johnie. I think that was a HUGE part of today - wanting to establish and confirm that bond with that friend......which can be looked at in different perspectives....so I see a smiling happy guy now - so hopefully that will last!

Mom: This letter is describing a behavior of Johnie's that I am not familiar with and yet the staff was describing something similar last year. Please read.

Teacher (last year): Johnie has formed a friendship with another student, but he is resistant to feedback about how he is trying to maintain the friendship. In a way he is trying to almost become the other student by copying his mannerisms, stating that the same things that bother the other student now bother him, etc.

Mom: After I read this letter, I spoke with both boys and the other mother. He does not appear to have this type of behavior outside the school. He is usually very self-centered. He thinks more about himself than anyone else. What do you think this means?

Social worker: You have here two very independent observations showing that the boy has poor ego-boundaries.

Mom: This years observation appears innocent enough until the social worker insists that it shows that Johnie has "poor ego-boundaries." Since I know my son well enough to know that he does not have "poor ego-boundaries," I have to figure out what is really happening here. I look at the facts and I see something odd. If this is two very independent observations, why does the teacher this year say "which can be looked at in different perspectives?" Now, I have to question why the teacher would make this statement? She would not say that if she was just making a casual observation. She wrote that observation with the clear intent of looking for something. She no longer appears to be making an independent observation. Suddenly, she appears to be looking for something specific.

If you bully a kid for not understanding, you will create a kid who appears to have poor ego-boundaries. If you put a kid with autism into a spontaneous game of kickball with a bunch of bullies, you will create a kid who appears to have poor ego-boundaries.

I did not in a million years want to imagine that the staff would be purposefully, willing to admit that they were bullying my son. However, when I researched poor ego-boundaries, I began to realize that staff was describing a child who is being bullied. WHY? As I continued my research on poor ego-boundaries, I discovered that psychosis is a sign of poor ego-boundaries. There it is. District is still unwilling to admit their mistakes. Oh god! When will this all end? Either the staff is trying to bully my son to make it look like he has behavioral problems, or they are trying desperately to show that he has signs of psychosis, when he never has. Neither situation looks at all like a safe place for Johnie and I immediately took him out of school and got homework for him.

Mom (to teacher): I know that Johnie does not have poor ego-boundaries.

I know that his ego suffers a great deal more at school than it does anywhere else.

I know that the social worker has an inaccurate perception of Johnie.

What do I do?

Teacher (to mom): The social worker is one of the most astute mental health providers that I have had the privilege of working with in this district.

Mom: I agree. I wasn't talking about the social worker. I was talking about my son. What do I do?

Mom (to social worker): Please may I have a detailed report explaining exactly how you came to the conclusion that Johnie has poor ego-boundaries.

Social worker: I would like to respond to the issue of ego boundaries. I am aware that this was initially brought to your attention last year. This was just sharing the observations we were making for your information. As a parent, you have every right to disregard that information or not. Our intention was to just share the information with you. The issue of ego boundaries does not change how he is programmed for in this school.

All this really creepy stuff has caused me to feel like double checking everything. Why is this happening???

I went to check Johnie's file. That is when I discovered that the diagnostic assessment done by the Autism Team four years ago, was different than what I had received.

Johnie appears to be struggling with respect to family issues, in an ongoing manner, and he describes some confusion in regard to his mother's involvement. Specifically, it is clear that his mother struggles with trust in regard to the school system. Further, it appears that Myrrena Schwegmann, in her effort to be helpful to Johnie, may get involved in his 'world' vis-a-vis the school in a way which may complicate things for him in terms of sorting out boundaries. In turn, the conflicts between home and school tend to be problematic in terms of sorting out Johnie's needs.

Now we are beginning to see why some of the creepy stuff is happening. I'm beginning to see why the staff is angry at me when I often have no idea what I may have done. Now we know why the staff is treating Johnie so poorly, and why we have all, each and every one of us involved in working with Johnie at school, have suffered with stress and confusion. This was not intended to be an assessment of Johnie. It was intended to create discension. It just gets creepier and creepier.

The principal of the school threatens truancy court and I explained that I cannot send my son to this school unless the staff is working with a child who has autism, not SED. At this point, staff is just bullying Johnie and openly admitting it. The principal promised improvements and there were no behavioral problems for the rest of the school year.

THE SED LABEL ON THE IEP

I have spent the last five years trying very hard to explain that Johnie does not fit the SED label on the IEP. I tried to convince teachers to observe Johnie outside the school. I even tried to hire a teacher to observe him outside the school. No takers. I brought testimonials from fifty friends to indicate that he does not fit the label. Nothing has worked. Nobody listened. This year, I called everyone I knew who might be able to attend the meeting, to please come support Johnie. Six friends came in support and district finally agreed to take the SED label off the IEP.

ASSESSMENT DATA FOR SOCIAL/EMOTIONAL/BEHAVIORAL

Johnie is a 13 year old student in the 8th grade who is eligible for special education and related services under the disability categories of Autism Spectrum Disorder as well as Significant Emotional Disability.

Mom: This IEP meeting took two days. Upon our return to the second meeting, not only is the SED label off the IEP, but they have suddenly cured Johnie of his ASD. Now they insist on labeling the IEP as physical - other. RED FLAG

Johnie has demonstrated the ability to socialize with his peers, form and maintain friendships with both his classmates and trusting adults, RED FLAG

Mom: Why should Johnie have difficulty trusting adults?

and manage the academic demands placed on him. RED FLAG

Mom: Since I showed this staff several times that Johnie does not have problems with "academic demands", until he is being graded on his disability rather than his ability, this is purely an attempt to protect themselves.

Johnie holds a healthy image of himself and expresses confidence in his ability to make decisions and preform tasks independently.

Mom: Which means he does not have poor ego boundaries.

According to Johnie's teachers, he displays low amounts of externalizing behaviors.

Mom: Which means he has never displayed any of the following behaviors described next.

His levels of hyperactivity, aggression, and conduct behaviors are well under control. RED FLAG

Mom: Unless staff wants to admit they have been teaching Johnie things they should not be.

They did report varying levels of anxiety, depression, withdrawal, and atypicality, which should be monitored in the future. RED FLAG

Mom: Indeed, this should always be reported because this shows all the signs of a child who is being bullied and I certainly do not understand why the staff at every school would want to show off about bullying Johnie.

Assessments were recommended to gather more information with respect to Johnie's pragmatic-language skills and written language skills.

Based on formal and informal assessments, Johnie demonstrates age appropriate pragmatic language usage. Relative areas of weakness in Johnie's pragmatic language skills do not prevent him from receiving reasonable educational benefit from regular education. RED FLAG

Mom: We need to get an independent assessment done for language pragmatics because Johnie has been bullied, harassed, misplaced and constantly misunderstood for years for not understanding many things presented socially and academically in school. District agrees to pay for an independent assessment for language pragmatics.

Johnie's composite score on the Contrived Writing Composite was in the average range....However, in his spontaneous writing sample, he did not demonstrate the ability to generalize these skills into his story. For the vocabulary subtest, the test taker is asked to write a sentence that incorporates a stimulus word. Although Johnie appeared to have receptive understanding of the vocabulary, he had difficulty using the stimulus word in a grammatically correct sentence. It should also be noted that Johnie's penmanship was difficult to decipher. He was also lacking many of the expected writing conventions. He demonstrated a lack of multiple paragraphs, appropriate end punctuation, capitalization and the use of complex sentence structure. He also struggled with the story's plot. His writing style and vocabulary level lacked maturity.

Mom: I have been trying to explain for years now, that Johnie does not know how to generalize his knowledge. The goals on most of his IEPs, included "Using proper spacing, capitalization and punctuation for written assignments." There has been no progress on these goals because Johnie does not understand the importance.

Goals on most IEPs are unused and unattended to.
Quarterly rubrics are written only once in all these years. RED FLAG

WHY does Johnie who was an obvious GIFTED WRITER in second grade, turn out to be UNABLE TO WRITE A PROPER SENTENCE by the time he starts ninth grade? RED FLAG

It is certainly not from a lack of trying on his part. Our home is filled with books and stories he has written over the years. Their just not publishable because he never learned HOW to write it down in the proper way. It is also shocking to note that this school district is supposed to be one of the best in the country.

Dear Executive Director:

Can you please explain a couple of questions I have?

How can you determine that Johnie has ASD for two years and then not on the third, when ASD is a permanent disability?

How can you make that determination based on the fact that he has friends?

It takes a lot more than that to make a determination for ASD. Please explain.

Executive Director writes:
The IEP team makes the determination of disability based upon the multidisciplinary assessment. Following the initial eligibility, this determination must be remade at least every three years. As per our agreement, an IEE is also part of our consideration.

Dear Advocate:

I sent this letter to the Executive Director and here is his response. Johnie made a lot of friends last year and so did all of his friends. As I am friends with all the mothers, we are all in shock that Johnie's IEP label was changed "because he made friends" and none of the other boys had the same change. I don't want to keep pointing out the obvious blunders here, but the staff at Johnie's next school is not going to understand all of his needs the way in which this is written.

After this meeting, I did several things to try to solve the confusion. First, I called the complaint department at the hospital where Johnie was misdiagnosed the first three times. I explained everything, including the horrors that Johnie has had to endure all these years in the schools from being misdiagnosed, misunderstood, and misplaced. I explained that Johnie had seen a a specialist who diagnosed him with Asperger's Syndrome and that the district ignored it. I asked if the hospital could reassess Johnie, not only so that they have a record of what has happened here, but maybe the district will listen to them. Hospital personnel were so horrified by what the district was doing to Johnie, that they agreed to provide a new diagnosis before school started.

I then set up a mediation with district and many things were brought to the table including a need for a new IEP, but one thing had a most striking impact. I discovered a different way of looking at the IEP and asked district personnel why the teachers in five different schools would show off about bullying a special needs boy? I have explained every year and at every IEP meeting that what is written on the SED page does not describe Johnie at all. Not even close. No. They are describing all the symptoms of a boy who is being bullied.

On the Determination of Disability page of every IEP, I tried to explain over and over again that Johnie just does not fit the criteria for the SIED label. He just does not have a behavioral problem. What they were describing was a kid that does not exist, and I said it every year. Here are the behaviors that have been reported on that page of the IEP's. **Please note**: A couple of the behaviors are obviously autistic features.

- Third grade IEP
* Exhibits pervasive sad effect, depression, and feelings of worthlessness; cries suddenly or frequently.
* Excessive fear and anxiety.
* Persistent physical complaints not due to a medical condition.
* Out of touch with reality, has auditory and visual hallucinations, thought disorders, disorientation, or delusions.
* Cannot get mind off certain thoughts or ideas, cannot keep self from engaging in repetitive and/or useless actions.
* Persistent patterns of bizarre and/or exaggerated behavior reactions to routine environments.

– Fourth grade IEP
* Excessive fear and anxiety.
* Out of touch with reality, has auditory and visual hallucinations, thought disorders, disorientation, or delusions.
* Cannot get mind off certain thoughts or ideas; cannot keep self from engaging in repetitive and/or useless actions.

– Fifth grade IEP
* Exhibits pervasive sad effect, depression, and feelings of worthlessness; cries suddenly or frequently.
* Displays unexpected and atypical affect for the situation.
* Excessive fear and anxiety.
* Persistent physical complaints not due to a medical condition.
* Exhibits withdrawal, avoidance of social interaction, and/or lack of personal care to an extent that maintenance of satisfactory interpersonal relationship is prevented.
* Out of touch with reality; has auditory and visual hallucinations, thought disorders, disorientation, or delusions.
* Cannot get mind off certain thoughts or ideas; cannot keep self from engaging in repetitive and/or useless actions.

– Sixth grade IEP
* Displays unexpected and atypical affect for the situation.
* Excessive fear and anxiety.
* Exhibits withdrawal, avoidance of social interaction, and/or lack of personal care to an extent that maintenance of satisfactory interpersonal relationship is prevented.

– Seventh grade IEP
* Displays unexpected and atypical affect for the situation.
* Excessive fear and anxiety.
* Exhibits withdrawal, avoidance of social interaction, and/or lack of personal care to an extent that maintenance of satisfactory interpersonal relationship is prevented.

– Eighth grade IEP
* Displays unexpected and atypical affect for the situation.
* Excessive fear and anxiety.
* Exhibits withdrawal, avoidance of social interaction, and/or lack of personal care to an extent that maintenance of satisfactory interpersonal relationship is prevented.

– Ninth grade IEP
No SED page, but staff still insisted on writing the following behaviors. "Staff did report varying levels of anxiety, depression, withdrawal, and atypicality, which should be monitored in the future."

My observations show that these teachers have been verbally and emotionally abusing my son all these years and showing off about it.

Emotional Abuse: Signs and Symptoms

- Feeling of depression
- Withdrawal from social interaction
- Isolation from friends and family
- Low self-esteem
- Fearfulness
- Increased anxiety
- Guilty feeling
- Feeling of shame
- Mood changes
- Nervous feeling
- Not trusting others
- Frequent blaming on others
- Self-blaming
- Pessimistic behavior
- Substance or drug abuse
- Extreme dependence on others
- Avoiding eye-contact
- Telling lies
- Aggressive behavior
- Emotional instability
- Suicidal attempts

If the emotional abuse remains unchecked, it can worsen the symptoms and may lead to serious emotional and psychological disorders. In some jurisdictions, failure to report child abuse cases are punished either by imprisonment or in the form of fine.

District reaction was to create something akin to a miracle.

The impact of this miracle on Johnie was such a huge relief. He felt more comfortable with the teachers in the following year of school than he had in more than five years. The one big problem? He had very little idea of how to communicate with teachers after all the years of verbal abuse. Why were many of the teachers so mean to him all those years? RED FLAG

I was invited to a six week class for the families of kids with special needs. There were quite a few reasons I was glad I had attended, despite having many years experience already. It was in many ways very informative. I wish this class had been a requirement before I went to my first IEP. It would have saved me from quite a bit of confusion. For one thing, I did not realize that Johnie had spent three years in classrooms that had a "modified" curriculum. Johnie and I would have been spared a whole lot of grief if we had understood and been able to avoid those classrooms. It was eye opening to note that I was not alone with the horrors I have experienced in the special needs program of this district. Many families were there, sharing their own experiences and some could not even speak English. What struck me as most alarming in these classes is when the SLP (Speech Language Pathologist) from the Autism Team got up and announced how proud she was that this district had gotten a language pragmatic teaching program in January of 2008. By then, Johnie had suffered for two years with communication difficulties which district had claimed was behavioral. Sometimes, school districts simply do not want to admit that they do not have the services or the properly trained staff in place. If they blame the kid, at least they don't look bad. RED FLAG

SECOND IEP MEETING

Johnie was in school for a month by the time we had this meeting. Two new diagnostics were brought to the table and one of the doctors were on the phone for the first hour of the meeting.

First diagnosis indicates - Asperger's Syndrome

Second diagnosis indicates - Semantic Pragmatic Disorder with Autism

                       - Mixed receptive-expressive language disorder

                       - Asperger's Syndrome

Right after the doctor got off the phone, staff were attempting to show me that Johnie does not fit the criteria for an autism spectrum disorder. I was overwhelmed with horror because I had tried so hard to prevent this confusion. By the time it was over, I was in tears, knowing that Johnie was going to be subjected to some kind of ill treatment in this school year too. Even though I tried very hard to show how Johnie fit all the criteria, I was overruled 20 to 1 and they wrote on the IEP, "In respect to current functioning, the team including the mom and her advocate concluded that Johnie did not meet the criteria for Autism Spectrum Disorder according to IDEA. RED FLAG

Mom: I have never agreed with the IEP team in all these years, knowing that Johnie has suffered with all the misunderstandings in this district. Even though he has all the clear signs of ASD, again I am forced to show all the obvious to the staff at this school.

The criteria for an Autism Spectrum Disorder according to IDEA is:

(All three of the following shall be documented)

QUALITATIVE IMPAIRMENT IN SOCIAL INTERACTION

(DOCUMENTED ON IEP)

Teacher: Would like to see Johnie more engaged with other students in the classroom. Seems like he needs strategies to start conversations with peers that are engaging but appropriate.

Teacher: He is usually the quietest person in the group and can tend to perseverate on science fiction topics, which turns other students off.

QUALITATIVE IMPAIRMENT IN COMMUNICATION

(DOCUMENTED ON IEP)

IEP team has agreed that Johnie qualifies for the SLI (Speech/Language Impairment)

Ironically, I recommended this three years ago and the team said he did not qualify.

RESTRICTED,REPETITIVE AND STEREOTYPED PATTERNS OF BEHAVIOR, INTERESTS, AND ACTIVITIES

(DOCUMENTED ON IEP)

Teacher: I know that some people with autism perseverate on specific topics, and Johnie certainly does that with technology, science fiction, and anything having to do with computer/video games.

Mom: because the staff was arguing about the ASD label, they certainly couldn't write this verbatim on the IEP. They changed it to read:

Teacher: Johnie can perseverate on the topics of technology, science fiction, and anything having to do with computer/video games.

THE ADVOCATE

Before Johnie had started eighth grade, I had sent out numerous letters to the advocate and the social worker expressing my concern in putting him in either school of choice. Both schools had presented very creepy scenarios that I did not want to put Johnie back into. In the end, I chose to accept the school who had promised improvements. Later, The advocate, social worker and I had a meeting in which the advocate and social worker accused me of sabotaging the IEP meeting and thinking for Johnie instead of allowing him to think independently.

Mom: Did I "sabotage" the meeting? I am still at a loss as to how I did that. I do not work in the school system and I am still just a mom. Johnie and I think entirely differently. If he had his way, he would have been sent to the other school. I also feel his fear and his pain and I react, to protect. When he does not see the point or is feeling hopeless, I will react because I care enough to do so. That does not mean that we always see eye to eye.

Who is the advocate, advocating for?

Shortly after this, the social worker asked me, "Why don't you fire your advocate?"

Mom: "Why should I?"

Why is he getting involved? What is his purpose?

In the past four years, I have felt that I really did not have much of an advocate. The advocate wasn't mean. She showed up to every meeting and always made a few comments. She just wasn't ever there for the boy. She did not always answer important emails or take any kind of action when I explained how things were terribly amiss. I expected that the advocate was a very busy person, so I generally did as much work as I could do on my own and only called the advocate when it was an important meeting. This was a mistake in itself because, by the time I called the advocate for another meeting, she was sometimes confused by the details of Johnie's needs.

While Johnie was attending eighth grade, it appeared as if the social worker was trying to get me and my advocate, mad at each other. Every time the advocate argued with me (something she never had done before that year), the social worker was present. Even at the IEP meeting that summer, the advocate was arguing with me about the label on the IEP (how weird is that). Then, the social worker would later ask me why I don't fire my advocate. WHY? What is he doing?

Later that summer, the advocate and I met with district personnel. That is when I pointed out that the IEP's are all documenting that the staff are bullying Johnie. The advocate asked me why I said that. I explained that the staff at every school often got angry at Johnie in spite of the fact that he does not understand language pragmatics. That is why he needs to be retested. The advocate turned to district personnel and said, "She thought of that all on her own." The advocate did not turn to me and say, "Good job!" No. The advocate wasn't talking to me at all. That made me feel sad. It revealed quite clearly that we were not working as a team.

After the IEP was done on Johnie, I went to look through his file to see if there was anything I did not

have. Sure enough, there was. It included two letters that I had written personally to the advocate. That was weird. They should not be in the boys school file. I finally realized that the social worker (at the previous school), was the only person who could have put those letters into the file. I had let him read all of my letters about a year and a half ago. Of the hundreds of letters he had access to, why those?

WHY? Why put those letters into the boys school file? What purpose does it serve?

I was at a total loss. I had no idea what to do except to go to the advocates supervisor. I had taken pictures of the letters, to show their placement in the file. I showed how poorly the IEP was written and explained how my efforts appeared fruitless with no support. The supervisor could plainly see that the IEP was a mess and came to the conclusion that sometimes people do not communicate well. (I did not see how that could possibly be the problem as I have hundreds of letters that I have written over the years explaining and verifying all the details of our case, but I held my tongue.) The supervisor suggested that I might need a lawyer, but I could not afford a lawyer. I do not like to fight either. I just want Johnie's needs met in school. So, the supervisor set me up with a new advocate.

NINTH GRADE

Dear Teacher: I am hoping you can accept in your heart that Johnie is a good boy but he may be a bit of a challenge in your classroom. His desire to learn and be able to further his education in college will keep him going. Your support and understanding will make it that much more successful.

Please know:

- He will have difficulty with handwriting and taking notes.
- He will have difficulties with organization.
- He may have difficulties in a group or team situation.
- He may have difficulties knowing what to focus on.
- He may have difficulties functioning if your class is loud and rowdy.
- He may shut down and be unable to function if anyone gets angry at him.
- He may have difficulties knowing how to express himself or asking what you mean.
- If he does not understand the significance, he may refuse to do it or just do it his way.
- Giving him firm expectations without judgments, helps him learn and succeed.
- Continual reassurance and constant guidance will reduce any potential stress.

Dear teachers: I am quite pleased to see how Johnie is progressing so far in all your classes. However, we did discover at least one homework assignment that got lost in translation. This is a common problem with Johnie, so please may I offer a suggestion. An assignment that is just a worksheet, would be easy for him to understand how to complete. If the assignment has multi levels of completion, he may get lost in translation and have very little comprehension of your expectations. Please can you help him by writing a detailed list.

Example: Book report

- Pick out a book of choice from the library.
- The book needs to be read by _____ date.
- Choose from the list, the type of book report you would like to do.
- Explain expectations in detail (how many pages, typed or hand written, layout, capitalization and punctuation, rough draft done by ___ date, etc.)
- Written report should be done by ___ date.
- Writing the details help the boy know your expectations, helps him refer back to the list should he forget some details and gives him the capability of doing a better job.

Dear IEP staff: I want to thank you all for doing your best to create a proper IEP for Johnie. I do have some questions though.

1. If Johnie does not fit the criteria for a qualitative impairment in social interaction, why have several of his teachers documented that impairment in this IEP?

2. If Johnie does not fit the criteria for a qualitative impairment in communication, why have we all agreed to document his need for a new label of a speech/language disability on this IEP?

3. If Johnie does not fit the criteria for a restricted, repetitive and stereotyped pattern of behavior, why is it documented on this IEP?

Case manager: As the team spoke about earlier, your questions are "Due Process" issues. Please contact the district if you would like to contest the IEP.

The lawyer that I went to consult, stated that staff created the IEP and should answer any and all questions concerning it that I may have.

Teacher: I asked Johnie what happened on Friday and he said that he and another boy were sitting next to each other in the computer lab. The other boy was messing around with his mouse and he told the boy to knock it off, there was some physical messing around. I know the other boy and think the situation was probably benign. A goal I would have for Johnie is to be able to negotiate these kinds of "guy messing around situations", without involving us adults.

Mom: To Johnie, or any kid with an autism spectrum disorder, it is not "benign", until he learns HOW to be able to stand up for himself. It is not "benign" until Johnie knows the difference between "horsing around" and real bullying. It is not "benign" until Johnie is actually learning the social skills he needs to help him feel safe in situations like this that can be interpreted in multiple ways.

Teacher: Thank you, I agree.

Teacher: I am Johnie's new teacher and wanted to touch base with you regarding his grade. As I suspected, most of the assignments that were missing, were actually done. He just hadn't turned them in. I helped him submit them electronically today. We need to work out a plan for him to follow through and get work completed. His materials for class seem to be in a bit of disarray, perhaps we can work together to help him with organization.

Mom: I am glad you were able to help Johnie learn how to turn in his homework. I tried to tell the staff at the IEP meeting how bad his organization was, but nobody seemed to think he needed more than a little help now and then. Johnie needs extensive training on how, why and the value of organization. He is just not AWARE organizationally. I do not know how I can help you without the team working on it all together. I have tried numerous times to do it on my own or offer the suggested need and I just get a brick wall. How can I help?

Monthly meetings were set up so that the IEP team could get together with Johnie and I to make sure that his needs are met.

November: Johnie will carry a notebook for teachers to write in daily, ask teachers to write in it daily. The teachers will check in with Johnie daily, write in the book daily.

The notebook "vanished" after two weeks and reappeared when school ended. I made a new one right away but no one ever used it.

December: Johnie will communicate better with teachers to understand work and when it is due.

Johnie will remember to give the teachers the back and forth book to sign.

Johnie will ask for clarification when he does not understand guidance.

Johnie will be supported in accessing missing assignments.

Johnie will find someone to tell if he is bullied or uncomfortable by situations.

Johnie grades reflect mostly As and F's and very little in between. He appears to be doing well until there are miscommunications and misunderstandings.

Johnie is overwhelmed by all our suggestions and expectations of him.

Mom: Can you please find a time where we can do an IEP review?

Case Manager: Since the team determined at the December progress check meeting that Johnie was making progress, we should wait until after the February meeting before scheduling an IEP review meeting.

Mom: A child receiving numerous "F's" in most of his classes is not a sign of progress. That is a sign that something is seriously wrong. Johnie's grades have always been pretty good over the years. When school started, his grades were all "As". Now they are going down hill. That is not a sign of progress. Please can we meet as soon as possible to resolve this dilemma? Thanks.

Teacher: Currently, Johnie has 7 zeros in class because he has not completed the work and turned it in.

Mom: Johnie had no problem finishing the work you sent home. I know he has the potential for giftedness and loves to learn, so I know it is not the work he is avoiding. Please can you tell me HOW Johnie got so far behind in the class? Thanks again for giving him all the assignments to catch up.

Case Manager: Johnie's teachers all report that he does not seem to want to accept assistance and has chosen to leave work incomplete and uncorrected. He has been offered opportunities for support and has not taken advantage of them. Thank you for working with him at home. Please encourage him to accept support from the teachers.

Mom: Do not pin the blame on Johnie. He is the one with special needs.

　　I showed you that it is not the work that he is avoiding.

　　I showed you that he is being graded on his disability rather than his abilities.

　　I showed you that he has Asperger's Syndrome and a language disability.

　　I showed you that he is and always has been gifted.

　　These are the things you have ignored to put the boy in the position of being unable to speak
　　 for himself.

　　That is why it is so important to write the IEP correctly.

I showed district director and Johnie's case manager that the first two IEP's indicated that he was in a gifted program. They said that Johnie's schedule for next year could be changed for him to attend accelerated classes.

WHAT?

I spent the better part of six years trying to show that my son is gifted and every single person who was involved in the IEP process has tried to deny it....until I showed that it was written there, right on the IEP.

I spent the better part of six years showing that you can't put an autistic child into a BD program. It is literally an unsafe environment for them to be in for many reasons. Most obvious was that, not only is he being bullied by his peers with no support, understanding, or lessons that he could understand, but the teachers are suddenly given permission to bully him too. It did not stop until I asked why the teachers would show off about doing that. Yup, there it is, written right on the IEP. All the obvious signs of a child being bullied, and nobody was doing anything about it for five long years.

Johnie did not receive a free appropriate public education as defined by the IDEA rules in all these years, because of the blatantly obvious errors that are written right on one IEP after the next.

The other big problem we had was the assessment done by The Autism Team (in fourth grade). It was done emotionally, not professionally. You can see it by the very words they write. It wasn't about the boy or me. That assessment that was created by the Autism Team, caused many people in this district over the years to act emotionally rather than professionally. That is why Johnie and I kept running. This is why Johnie kept running from classes and I kept pulling him out of one school after the next. The emotions, the commotion, did not have anything to do with us.

I tried to send in a state complaint, but they would not accept the way in which I wrote it. They do not accept a complaint beyond one year. I could not figure out HOW to keep it all in one year.

I thought about Due Process and possibly a lawsuit many times. First of all, as a single mother, I am limited in funds for these types of situations. Who has the time for that anyway? Ultimately, I have always had faith that their has got to be a better way of resolving these situations. I don't like to fight. I like to resolve things and as a result, I had set up many, many meeting over the years.

Finally, this last meeting where district and the school had finally accepted the fact that Johnie should be in accelerated classes, was the last straw. It wasn't about him anymore. It was about what was written on the IEP. Where was the human element? Who was actually paying attention to Johnie? They are not even thinking of the fact that Johnie has lost so much academically because of being misplaced, that he may not even be capable of accelerated classes by now. Who knows? I finally gave up on putting Johnie in this school district ever again after that. Ironically, we have decided to go virtual to get closer to the human element that we both appreciate so much more than we have experienced in this school district.

Teacher: Johnie's monthly meeting will be coming up soon. Please complete a faculty feedback form and plan to attend. Also, if you are willing, please plan to attend his IEP review in August.

Mom: Frankly, I don't see the point of attending these meetings. Somehow it never appears to be about Johnie or his needs. My advocate and I cannot attend.

District: We discussed having the next monthly meeting in May as well as setting up an IEP review in August. Your message below seems to indicate that you and your advocate have decided not to meet. Is that correct? Please respond via email so we have written documentation. Thank you.

Mom: Frankly, I don't see the point of attending these meetings. Somehow it never appears to be about Johnie or his needs. My advocate and I cannot attend.

District: Thank you for making it clear that you and your advocate cannot attend the monthly meeting. Now the team needs a clear understanding of your intent for the IEP review that was requested and set aside in August. Do you still intend to have this requested meeting? Please indicate via email.

Mom: Frankly, I don't see the point of attending these meetings. Somehow it never appears to be about Johnie or his needs. My advocate and I cannot attend.

District: I am sorry I do not understand your intent. Please be very specific. Do you want the team to cancel the meeting in August? Thank you.

HOPE AND PRAYERS FOR THE FUTURE

The executive director writes:

I would like to hear from parents who may have problems, challenges, or needs assistance in obtaining support and services for their child in this school district. If parents have solutions to the problems they are facing please include that in your letter as well. The district would like to advance teacher's instruction in order to support students who learn differently. You can be the voice of change.

Parent writes:

I am very glad to see that you are seeking improvement in support and services in your school district. CDE (Department of Education) has sent out questionnaires on the support and services in your district randomly but I really doubt they portrayed an accurate depiction. I never received a questionnaire in the seven years my son had an IEP.

I have written hundreds of letters over the years trying very hard to suggest improvements that can be made. We wanted so much for my son to have the same great education that my daughter had received with the support and services that he needed, but nobody seemed to be interested in providing that and we finally had to pull my son out of your district.

Here are just a few of the suggestions I have made over the years.

1. All parents who have children with special needs should get some kind of training before they commit to their first 504 or IEP meeting. They need to be fully informed of their options.

    A) CDE has an excellent training video that they have recently created. I recommend that new parents be ready to take notes because it is an overwhelming amount of information to consume.

    B) SEAC created an excellent six week course that would be easier for a new parent to handle. Unfortunately, I never heard of any training till we had struggled through for six years.

2. If the district is willing and able to pay for an independent diagnostic evaluation:

    A) Make sure your director knows where to find appropriate sources and can provide three different names and numbers that are up to date and accurate.

    B) Make sure that your director is not hiring that one source (that is all she provided us), to create a false and misleading document.

    C) Should this happen, you really need someone in district who knows how to read diagnostics and can easily read that the diagnosis was not intended to show the needs of the boy.

3. I need to recommend that your Autism Team really needs more training on how to create a proper assessment of a child.

    A) They should have an understanding of how to read diagnostics.

    B) They need to be able to get a history on the child which includes school and home.

    C) They need to be able to explain the boys needs rather than his diagnostics.

    D) The assessment done on my son, appears to be written as a personal vendetta. It is not written professionally to describe his needs. The Autism Team needs to learn how to write a professional assessment and the rest of the district personnel needs to be able to read the difference.

    E) If you are going to have a crew working as part of the Autism Team, they really need to understand the needs of a child with autism. They all need to understand why it is so inappropriate to put an autistic child into a BD/SED program. They need to understand the vast difference in needs.

F) Make sure they understand the IDEA rules for assessing a child.

4. I recommend that staffing in all your schools be well trained in how to write an IEP. I have 9 IEP's written in 6 different schools and not one of them are written according to the IDEA rules. This discrepancy caused a great deal of confusion and my son never got his needs met.

A) EXAMPLE: If the child gets a diagnosis for psychosis, he would obviously get a label of SIED on the IEP. However, if the child is in the Gifted/Talented program, shows no behavioral problems, and is very cooperative and compliant as written right on the IEP, he does not fit the SIED label. According to the IDEA rules, if he does not fit the criteria, than he cannot get the label.

B) In all the years my son was in your district, only once were the goals attended to. They need to be attended to daily and reported quarterly, like the grades. The affect of this situation caused my son, who has frequently been noted as a gifted writer, to be unable to write a proper sentence by the time he started ninth grade.

C) In an IEP meeting, I believe it is very important that only staffing who are trained in a particular area of concern should respond to that suggested service. Example: At our last meeting, I suggested that my son needs extensive training in organizational skills. It was you, who said he did not need the services even though you have no idea what my sons needs are and have no idea why he would have that need. The result of your decision, was that my son spent the entire year being graded on his disability rather than his abilities in class.

5. Your BD/SED programs in all of your schools (six that I know of), really need extensive change

A) I went to a meeting at the district offices once and a teacher had pointed out that she was so busy looking for poor behaviors that she forgot to notice the good behaviors. That was my sons experience for many years.

B) Because of our situation, I have met numerous boys who have a "dual" diagnosis of autism and SED. This is incredibly horrifying and inappropriate.

C) Your Autism Team needs to be trained in distinguishing the difference between the behaviors of a BD/SED student and/or an autistic student. This is so they can train the teachers in all your schools to be able to distinguish the difference. Example: BD students behaviors are action and autistic students behaviors are reaction.

D) While children with autism have a tendency of showing behaviors that can be alarming at times, they are not the same as a BD/SED child and should be handled entirely differently.

E) Even though my son is a well behaved child, he is autistic and very naive because of it. He was often learning poor behaviors from his peers and his teachers and/or reacting to the behaviors around him. He was also learning to associate stress with academics which is why I had to keep pulling him out of one school after the next to teach him at home.

F) While all of your BD/SED programs make a point of noting the childs behaviors, not one of them have ever pointed out WHY the behavior was happening. No one has ever explained what happened before or what caused the behavior to happen. Behaviors happen for a reason and that needs to be explained for the problem to improve.

G) A child with high-functioning autism needs completely different support and services than a BD/SED child. Example: A child with ASD will generally have an average to above average academic capability. Because of this, he should never be put into modified classes. It will cause them unnecessary stress because they need to know they are accomplishing something. Generally speaking, a BD/SED student will not care about academics.

6. Let's take a look at the qualifications of my sons social skills and writing teacher for 9th grade.

A) She tested him on pragmatic language (TOPL-2) and her assessment was that he demonstrates age appropriate pragmatic language usage. Based on my sons experiences of being bullied and harassed for not understanding our language in these schools all these years, I had to insist that my son needed to be retested.

B) Was she doing an appropriate test? Was she reading it correctly? Is she qualified to be doing the testing? Three years previously, I pointed out that he needed the SLD (Speech Language Disability) label on his IEP and again, an "expert" was brought in to the IEP meeting who claimed that my son did not qualify. He speaks too clearly and his grades are too good.

C) My son was retested outside district and found to have far more needs than the teacher or the "expert" had registered on their tests. He was given an SLD label on the IEP to reflect that need but was never provided the support and services for that need. I suspect that no one at that school was qualified.

D) This teacher also tested my son on the test of Written Language - Fourth Edition (TOWL-4). She appeared to be far more qualified to test him in this area because it all appeared quite accurate. My son is indeed lacking knowledge in many areas of writing skills including the inability to generalize his knowledge and skills.

E) However, as his writing and social skills teacher, she never once attempted to help him learn how to generalize his knowledge. This requires a very open communication between teachers and parents, so that what he is learning in her writing class, he is also learning in all his classes. The social skills he is learning in school, he should be practicing at home.

F) This teacher was also most vocal about pointing out that my son was making friends. I know my son is friendly, but he needs support to be able to understand how to maintain a friendship so it is clear that this teacher is not being completely honest. It also became immediately apparent that she is not qualified to be teaching my son the social skills that he needs. First of all, the rest of the staff could see that he was not making friends and relayed that information right on the IEP. Second, if she was actually qualified, she would have worded it differently. She would have said, "He is able to make AND MAINTAIN friendships." which he is incapable of doing without the proper support and services.

G) Because she was not trained to be able to properly assess my sons needs, he did not receive the appropriate support and services that he needed. He was also unable to make any friends that year.

Your children in this district will be unable to receive the appropriate services as defined by the IDEA rules, unless the staff are properly trained.

Thanks,
Myrrena Schwegmann

UNDERSTANDING HIGH FUNCTIONING AUTISM

I was given a teachers guide from the boys first grade teacher. This guide clarified many things for me about the boy over the years. It helped me be able to work with the boy better than anyone could. It helped me stay focused and to never get confused about what the boys diagnosis and ultimately his needs were over the years. It helped keep me from getting confused when the doctors and teachers in the district were demonstrating their confusions. Although it was an excellent source of comfort and clarity, I had many other sources that have helped with clarity in areas that were not covered in that guide. I decided to create a guide that covers more details in a way that can be helpful and yet easy to access for us all. At least that is my intention here.

ASD (Aspergers Spectrum Disorder) is a neurological disorder which makes it very difficult to teach a child in the conventional way. The experts note that the key to understanding autism spectrum disorders is to recognize that it profoundly alters how these kids perceive their world. The following is suggestions for teachers and parents to help their child succeed. Every child is different, therefore these ideas are only given in the broadest sense. It is up to you to tailor these ideas to the individual child you are working with.

1. FEW INTERESTS

- They tend to focus on one interest to an extreme which can get uncomfortable and irritating to some people around them.
- Help them by suggesting times and lengths of time they can talk of their interest.
- Have them do assignments around their interest, but try to broaden their awareness and interests as you work with them.
- Assignments outside their interest should be given with very clear, very specific directions.

2. MINIMIZE TRANSITIONS

- A child with ASD may often have a tendency of feeling overwhelmed in a classroom if it is not highly structured.
- It is far easier for them to cope if they have very clear expectations.
- Transitions or changes in routine, need to be explained ahead of time. It is often difficult for them to assimilate that change or figure out how, which may cause behaviors from them at times.

- Providing choices may cause an overwhelmed and confused kid. This should only be done if it is part of the lesson and he is closely supervised.

3. REPETITIVE MANNERISMS OR STIMMING

- You might find the child lining up their toys at an early age, repeating words or phrases, rocking, pacing, hand flapping, jumping up and down, or perseverating on a topic of interest.
- To the average person, this appears to be a behavioral problem and there is a good chance that his peers will bully and tease him for it. It is best to educate his peers to understand that this is an important part of who he is.
- These mannerisms are all a very important part of self-soothing or de-stressing and helping them gain control of themselves in the incredibly confusing and overwhelming world that they live in.
- We also need to help them find an alternative to self-calming that will be accepted in our society.

4. SENSORY ISSUES

- These children are usually highly sensitive to taste, touch, smell, visual, and most prominently, auditory stimulation.
- Many behaviors are associated with sensory sensitivity.
- A child's sensory issues and their reaction needs to be clearly defined to then be able to help them learn to cope.
- To create an environment for them to work and live more comfortably in, is to focus on minimalism. The less clutter on the walls, tables, etc. the easier it is for them to know what to focus on.

5. POOR MOTOR COORDINATION

- These children may tend to be physically uncoordinated and unable to keep up with their peers. Competitive and team sports may not be a good idea without close supervision.
- Their physically awkward and ungainly abilities can lead to bullying and teasing by peers and needs to monitored closely.
- Their poor motor coordination can make it difficult to write and draw. They may need more time for written assignments and timed tests.
- They may need help getting notes.
- Assistive technology may be needed to decipher the writing.

6. GENERALIZATION

- These children tend to have a great difficulty understanding how to generalize their knowledge to other situations.
- Teachers and parents need to work together to make sure that the child has the same experiences and lessons in multiple situations.
- All social and/or behavioral lessons, organizational skills and assignments done at school, need to be worked on at home and in the community.

7. DISORGANIZATION

- It can be very difficult for these children to understand the relevance of being organized without very firm and clear guidelines.
- To help kids with ASD be able to learn to function independently as adults, it is important to teach them to rely on daily schedules.
- Some suggested ideas are: Create a list of classes for their notebook that details their needs for each class. Have a folder for each class. One side has the homework assignments to be done and the other side has the assignments that have been done.
- Highly recommend graphic organizers for math and writing. It helps keep the math problems organized in one place and helps keep his thoughts organized when planning out a written assignment.
- At home, it would be a good idea to keep a list of expectations and chores hung prominently. Even free time should be more structured for these kids so they have choices of things to do to avoid getting in trouble.

8. ACADEMICS

- They generally display an average to above average intelligence but lack the awareness and comprehension skills of their neurotypical peers.

- While they have the intelligence to join in regular education, they often do not have the emotional resources to cope with all of the demands in that classroom.
- They tend to get easily stressed and overwhelmed by their rigid thinking and/or needs. They can often can get self-critical and prone to depression if they are unable to attain teacher expectations.
- The teacher needs to be calm, predictable, and matter-of-fact. Their tone of voice may affect the child due to heightened sensory sensitivity.
- Teachers and/or clinicians often get blinded by the academic strengths of these children and forget to attend to their neurologically-based weaknesses.
- These children may have difficulties understanding intuitively.
- They may struggle with focusing on task, may get easily distracted or may be unclear on what they are supposed to focus on.
- It can be quite difficult for them to multi-task.
- They generally need step by step directions.
- Large assignments need to be broken down to small parts with very specific guidelines (written or typed, how many pages, paragraphs, how do you want it written, what are your specific expectations).
- Visual aids are most helpful.
- Make sure he is learning to generalize all lessons. Put it in writing so that it is concrete.
- Sometimes they tend to get lost and confused unless you teach "the parts before the whole".
- They tend to be literal and concrete thinkers. They love facts and figures. Computers are generally quite enjoyable and understandable.
- Abstractions, like metaphors, irony, jokes, emotional nuances, relationship issues, etc. may be difficult to comprehend.
- Very real difficulty understanding "Theory of mind".
- Problem solving skills tend to be quite poor.

9. SMALL CLASS SIZE

- It would be ideal to make sure these kids are in a smaller class size so they will experience less distractions and more individual attention.
- unfortunately, some school districts do not feel they can afford this unless the ASD child is placed in an SED program.
- Although these kids tend to react to their environment in such a way as to be labeled "behavioral", it is simply their expression of confusion and they should never be placed into a BD or SED program or classroom.

- In an SED program, kids with ASD will not be learning the social skills they need.
- They will not understand the behavioral lessons in this program, nor will they understand the behaviors of the teachers or their peers.
- The sensory stimulation in these programs are far more intense and usually more difficult for the sensitive child with ASD.
- Their peers will be far less intelligent and less inclined to want to learn.
- Their peers in an SED program will be more "streetwise" than the ASD child and he will inevitably be easily bullied.
- The teachers need to be more firm with the children in this type of program which can be quite a bit more frightening to a child with ASD.

10. SOCIAL SKILLS

- Most of these children would like to make friends. They usually have no clue how to go about doing that.
- Protect the child from bullying and teasing. They are usually too naive to understand how to protect themselves.
- Educate peers on ASD and their social awkwardness as a real disability.
- Praise peers when they are compassionate with him.
- Actively encourage child to socialize and provide guidance where and when needed (unstructured moments like lunch and recess).
- Social skills guidance a must. Their social judgment improves ONLY when they have been taught what their peers learn intuitively.
- Verbal skills often come out awkward. Sometimes they appear to have a brilliant understanding. At other times, they make up their own way of explaining which can appear odd or even psychotic if you are not remaining aware of their neurological deficits.
- Try not to ask him leading questions. He may get lost in comprehending your line of questioning and/or his literal interpretation.
- Generally, these kids will need access to a clear understanding of language pragmatics.
- They often have a very difficult time understanding "Theory of Mind". They usually do not understand how to comprehend other people (what they are thinking, what they mean, body language, non verbal cues, etc.), without clear guidelines.
- Teach awareness of body language, facial expressions, different emotions, what they look like and what they feel like.

- Teach them what to say, how to say it, how to say it different in different situations,etc.
- Visual aids are very helpful and/or have them role-play various situations.
- All social skills that are practiced at school, should also be practiced at home to incorporate the generalization skills and practice.

11. BEHAVIORS

- Behaviors of any kind are happening for a reason.
- Find out WHY the behavior is happening. (repetitive mannerisms? Sensory issues? Social issues? Bullying?)
- You may have to ask the parent (teacher). Have they experienced the same? How do they resolve it?
- If you are working with him in a calm, clear, and firm manner, he will more likely hear you and your guidance... even if it is much later when you have given him time to think it over.
- If you are stressed by his behaviors, he is even more stressed.

12. HOME/LIFE SKILLS

- Teach them WHY it is important to brush their teeth (or tie their shoes, button clothing, comb hair, clean up mess, go to the bathroom, answer the phone, etc). They generally do not "get it" without an explanation.
- If his motor skills weakness is making it difficult to do many tasks, help him build his strength, so that he can. Be gently persistent. Don't let him make excuses.
- Give them visual aids to explain step by step when needed.
- Keep a list of chores and/or things to do in easy access. Use it till it is a habit.
- Practice what to say and how to say things on the phone.
- For four years, mom and dad and many friends were unable to teach the boy how to ride a bike. Finally, mom thought about what she had read about needing to "Teach the parts before the whole", when working with kids who have high functioning autism. She bought him a pair of heelies and taught him to balance on his heels, rolling on wheels, steering, and finally skill.

Then she put him back on a bike and it was very easy for him to figure it out after that.
- Sometimes, teaching a kid with ASD is being able to "think outside the box."

TO A FURTHER UNDERSTANDING

I had an incredible support system outside the school district who was always there for me and Johnie when things got difficult. I cannot tell you how many times my clients were agreeable to a schedule change or accepting of my bringing Johnie to work with me because of all that he endured at the schools. Constantly, I spoke with family members about meetings I had gone to where I was bullied into listening to twenty people telling me they knew my son better than I did. Numerous times I spoke with neighbors about being yelled at or even ignored when I tried to explain Johnie's needs. Countless friends have patiently listened to me as I tried to comprehend why Johnie was being bullied by teachers. I have even questioned whether I may have caused the problems and confusion. Inevitably, I knew I never had. I never had a problem communicating with anyone outside the district.

The meetings at the schools were always charged with emotions which made it very difficult to make rational decisions. Even as I had pointed this out on numerous occasions, the problem remained. Having a fabulous support system outside the district, prevented me from losing the clarity that the meetings would invariably put into question. This created a record of consistency on my part, while the district shows great inconsistencies and confusion in every single meeting over the years.

Even though I was often accused (by the offenders) of being the problem, I knew I couldn't be. I had all the written evidence from professionals to show that I knew what I was talking about. I had my son diagnosed often to show that I knew his needs. I had the ECEA rules which encourages involvement in advocating for my son(2.33 Parent, 4.01 Parental consent, 4.03(7) Parental participation, 4.03(8) requirements for parental involvement, 6.01(3) Parent access to records, 6.01(8) Amendment of records at parent request) backing me up. I even had the capability of helping him learn his social and academic skills, far more efficiently and effectively than any teacher in the district could. I'm not a teacher either. I just know Johnie well, and I understand autism. However, I inevitably ran into obstacles from educators and school officials who ignored my guidance and suggestions and eventually my son's needs. It took me a long time to realize that the initial IEP done on Johnie was the source of most of our problems. 4.02 of the ECEA rules, which consists of the Child Identification Process, was essentially ignored all these years.

This district proudly proclaims a "Dedication to Excellence" on their stationary and yet I have been forced to question that. This book primarily consists of direct quotes from Johnie's IEPs, letters from teachers and other school forms. It also includes quotes from his diagnostics and other sources to show the inconsistencies in this district that does not bare any resemblance to a "dedication to excellence."

Johnie and two of his friends (that I know of), should have gotten the support and services for being "twice exceptional". That is.... gifted with a disability. They were all denied that right as defined by the ECEA rules #12.01 (22). Why? Just because they have autism?

Why was Johnie's giftedness ignored? Why were teachers telling me that Johnie was "avoiding the work" year after year, when he had no troubles doing it at home? Johnie's first and second grade teachers were capable of working with his strengths and weaknesses and yet few teachers were capable of distinguishing his needs after the first IEP was written on him. What was it that caused most of the teachers to be unable to see Johnie's potential after third grade? Why did I see no homework at all after third grade except in sixth grade? Where did it go? Even though I asked for it often, I was told it was "his responsibility." Even though the record shows that Johnie was extremely disorganized, somehow the work came home in sixth grade. The teachers make reference to a recycle bin in eighth grade where the kids could toss their work (see page 63). Johnie was so disorganized that he would not be able to think of using a recycle bin without clear guidelines, so I believe that they have helped Johnie keep his work from me all these years. Why? What were they hiding?

Johnie has been in six different schools in this district and only two teachers showed they actually had enough knowledge to be able to see Johnie's obvious high-functioning autism. His first grade teacher and his sixth grade language arts teacher. They were only capable of assessing Johnie's needs to a certain degree of their knowledge and/or qualifications. Unfortunately, as my paperwork shows, there were no other professionals working in this district who are qualified to assess Johnie's needs and yet they did anyway.

In eighth grade, (when district was finally forced to admit Johnie's autism), I kept asking for a professional to work with all the autistic boys in the school. They finally sent one for the second semester, who showed me her credentials with 20 years experience. She was very nice and helped the boys with their Life Skills. Unfortunately, she did not show an interested in working with Johnie's social needs when he clearly lacked the social understanding that any autistic boy does. You can see that by her statements (pages 64-65).

I do not believe that any of the other boys I met with autism in this district (a dozen or so) who were placed into an SED program, should have ever been placed there. It only made their situations worse, more confusing than ever for them, and none of them had their needs met in that environment. Over and over again, they were expected to "be accountable" for social situations they did not understand. How many other boys have been placed into that awful situation?

I have no choice but to question why this district and the Autism Team does not know better? I do not think for a minute that many of the people I worked with in this district were as stupid as they acted. I just have to question why? In the end, I must say that none of this had anything to do with a "dedication to excellence", and none of it has anything to do with Johnie and me. It is just an observation of how moral and ethical standards got lost in the system.

Johnie is safe now. He is doing school virtually. He finally has a wonderful speech teacher who is helping him learn how to understand our language. He would prefer to be in a regular school. There are a vast array of social skills that cannot be learned virtually. He does not understand how to interact with his neuro-typical peers. He does not understand how to interact with teachers because of his experiences in this district. He would like very much to be able to learn these things. He loves to learn.

Johnie recently wrote a paragraph assignment:

WHEN I GET HURT

When I get hurt, my heart turns corrupted depending on what type of hurt was inflicted upon myself. When I am hurt the pain recycles until it becomes pure and flows away. When I can control the pain then it's not too painful of a hurt. It becomes trapped inside my brain waiting to be swept away into the atmosphere harmlessly. When I am hurt, the pain will always go away.

Thanks to all who have written books and articles about Autism Spectrum Disorders, Asperger's Syndrome, high functioning autism, psychosis and its history with autism, etc. They have all helped mom avoid the confusion.

Karen Williams: "Understanding the Student With Asperger's Syndrome:Guidelines for Teachers"(O.A.S.I.S. web page)

Kerry Hogan: "TEACCH Autism Program; Recommendations for Students with High Functioning Autism" (teacch.com)

Tom Berney: "Asperger Syndrome From Childhood Into Adulthood" (apt.rcpsych.org)

(yourlittleprofessor.com)

Paramjit T. Joshi & Kenneth E. Towbin: "Psychosis in Childhood and it's Management"

Michael D. Powers: "Asperger Syndrome and Your Child"

Tony Attwood: "The Complete Guide to Asperger's Syndrome"

Temple Grandin: "Thinking in Pictures: My life With Autism", "The Way I See It"

Wendy Lawson: "The Passionate Mind"

John Elder Robinson: "Look Me in the Eye"

Daniel Tammet: "Born on a Blue Day"

Tom Page: "Parallel Play"

www.education-world.com : Are you a bully? By Linda Starr

Walt Disney's movie, "Lelo and Stitch – Stitch Has a Glitch"

www.ingramcontent.com/pod-product-compliance
Lightning Source LLC
Chambersburg PA
CBHW050417290526
45786CB00003B/1296